NADIA ANJUMAN

Smoke Drifts:
Selected Poems

translated from Persian by
Diana Arterian and Marina Omar

edited by Diana Arterian

introduction by Aria Aber

 WORLD POETRY

Smoke Drifts: Selected Poems
English translation copyright © Diana Arterian and Marina Omar, 2025
Introduction copyright © Aria Aber
Translators' Notes copyright © Diana Arterian and Marina Omar, 2025
Notes to the Poems copyright © Diana Arterian, 2025

Earlier versions of the translations in this book first appeared in the following journals: *Apogee, Arc Poetry Magazine, Arkansas International, Asymptote, Aufgabe, Brooklyn Rail, Circumference, Denver Quarterly, Eleven Eleven, Exchanges Journal, Gulf Coast, International Poetry Review, National Translation Month, North American Review, Poet Lore, Two Lines*.

First Edition, First Printing, 2025
ISBN 978-1-954218-38-3

World Poetry Books
New York, NY
www.worldpoetrybooks.com

World Poetry titles are distributed by Asterism Books (US) and Turnaround Publisher Services (UK). Subscriptions and standing orders are available from the publisher.

Library of Congress Control Number: 2025943372

Cover design by Andrew Bourne
Typesetting by Don't Look Now
Printed in Lithuania by BALTO Print

World Poetry Books is a 501(c)(3) nonprofit and registered charity founded in 2017 in New York City and a member of the Community of Literary Magazines and Presses (CLMP).

World Poetry's publications and programs are made possible by grants from the Poetry Foundation, Hawthornden Foundation, and the New York State Council on the Arts with the support of the Office of the Governor and the New York State Legislature, and supported by an affiliation with the Humanities Institute and the Translation Program at the University of Connecticut (Storrs), as well as individual donors and our subscribers. To learn more about supporting World Poetry, please visit our website: worldpoetrybooks.com/support.

Table of Contents

Introduction by Aria Aber   vii

In Vain   17
Peace   19
Red Majesty   21
Eternal Pit   23
Human, Stone, Iron   25
How   29
Bent   31
A Story   33
My Garden   37
Accept the Truth   39
Fresh Buds   45
Poison   47
My World   49
Go   53
Mountain, Sea   55
Drink! Drink!   59
Prison   63
Crazy Heart   67
Plaything   69
Bitter Stories   75
The Night of Poetry   77
The Sun of Knowledge   79
A Taste of Ghazal   81
Steel Strings   83
Flower of Smoke   85
Plea   87

I Wish   91
Fantasy   93
Broken   95
Unnoticed   97
Like Flint   101
The Sun's Lance   103
Bedroom   107
God-Given Beauty   111
Asleep in a Haze   113
Fake Smile   117
New Seeds   119
The Most Faded Word   121
The Moment   123
Escape   125
We Must Try   127
The Leaves of Patience   133
Turmoil   135
The Most Solemn Verse   139
If   141

Translators' Notes   143
Chronology   158
Notes to the Poems   160
Further Reading   169
Acknowledgments   170
Biographies   171

Aria Aber:
On Nadia Anjuman

The first time I encountered Nadia Anjuman was in 2015. I was living in London, and the photo I saw of her, hanging on the walls of my college campus on International Women's Day, haunted me. She is not smiling, her serious, aggrieved eyes stare at the camera; her head is covered by a tight headscarf. In the years that followed, I devoured her peculiar and powerful poems, often written in free verse—Shamloui, as they call it in Farsi, after the great poet Ahmad Shamlou. She wrote fiercely, with a formal deftness that bears witness to a profound respect for the canon and the motivation to reinvent tradition. And while her work circles the topics of womanhood—desire for touch, for beauty, for a life unimpeded by men—what moved me most was her insistence on the sacred power of poetry itself. Like other writers who wrote under political duress, such as Paul Celan or Federico García Lorca, almost every one of her poems, can be read as an ars poetica:

> My hostess, if you admire my poem
> invite me under the shade of a cypress tree
> Sit me on a rug of spangled clover
> and hand me two bunches of sweet basil*

I was a young, aspiring poet myself, hungry for history, for ancestry, for a tradition I could identify with. I had been looking for a writer like me: another Afghan woman. And I found it in Nadia Anjuman. She was a writer who had come before me. She was a poet

---

* From "In the Company of Spring's Daughter," tr. Diana Arterian and Marina Omar, InTranslation [The Brooklyn Rail], February 2015: https://intranslation.brooklynrail.org/persian-dari/poetry-by-nadia-anjuman/

of the country I was exiled from and was writing to and about. And if she addressed the reader across the page as her "hostess," then so was she mine. She was, there is no other way to say it, my kin.

Nadia Anjuman published her first book, *Gul-e-Dodi* (Flower of Smoke), in 2005. At a quarter-century old, she had lived a life entangled in the great ruins of imperial warfare. She was born a year after the Soviet invasion, witnessed the rise and fall of the Taliban and the beginning of the U.S. occupation that would eventually become the longest war in American history. During the years of the oppressive Taliban regime that foreclosed women's higher education, she studied literature and writing in secret at the famous Golden Needle Sewing School under the guidance of the professor Muhammad Ali Rahyab. Three times a week, about thirty women in long burqas met up at his residence under the pretense of learning how to sew—but beneath the fabrics and needles in their bags they carried books, pens, paper. They discussed Dostoevsky and Nabokov and Tolstoy while the children played outside in the courtyard. Those children would alert the adults in case the morality police came to check on them. If they had been caught, they would have been sentenced to death.

All this happened in Herat, the ancient city where she was born. Herat is known for its blue mosque, its ancient citadel, and its rich cultural heritage, which stretches back to the Avestan period. Literature is a part of the city's soul, its pride and power. The great Persian poet Rumi called it the "pleasantest of cities," the "Pearl of Khorasan." I am still impossibly moved by the fervor and dedication of these students and teachers, who risked their lives in the pursuit of literature, and, most of all, by the resilience of Nadia Anjuman. Like all great artists, she was possessed by a wayward ambition that altered the course of her life.

In a 2001 *New York Times* article on Herat, Amy Waldman describes Anjuman as follows:

Swathed in black, she curled up like a cat in her professor's study, black eyes peering from an elfin face. She is 20 years old and has written 60 or 70 poems.

As the first person in her family to love words, she has had to fight, like a number of Professor Rahyab's students, for her family's cooperation. She has fought, too, to stave off marriage, fearing it will limit her freedom to write. "I think I've been quite successful," she said. "Girls are expected to marry at 14 or 15." She writes mostly about women's lives, "because we have suffered a lot."

It's hard not to see the prescience of her words now. Three years later, Anjuman married a man who was, like her, a graduate of literature at Herat University. But rather than finding a true partner in him, he and his family denounced the publication *Gul-e-Dodi* for having brought shame upon the family. On November 5, 2005, just a few months after the publication of her first book, her husband beat her unconscious, and left her to die the most terrible death. According to Anjuman's brother, beatings were not uncommon in their marriage, and although her death is often called an "alleged honor killing," in reality, this femicide was the consequence of far more quotidian domestic violence. After her husband was arrested for her murder, Anjuman's father was pressured to forgive him to lessen his sentence, to which he relented. This led to a quick release, and the husband was granted custody of their young son. In the end, there was no real justice for Anjuman's heartbreaking death.

The tragic end to her short life manifested her fate as a martyr and made her a symbol of all Afghan women yearning to be free. Despite the circumstances, I hope that it isn't by her death that she will be defined, but rather by her poetry, as she writes in the ghazal "My Garden":

> In time my work will be legendary
> I will fill the chest of history with gold

> If Anjuman helps me write these verses
> I will gild every book with pure poetry

The power of Anjuman's language lies in the chemistry between thematic universality and imagistic inscrutability. While her poems often draw on traditional forms, such as the ghazal, and classic Persian symbols, such as birds, fire, pomegranates, and flowers, they also demonstrate an original vision. The work cannot be read through a confessional or autobiographical lens; there is a hermetic intelligence infusing it. The speaker seems to emerge from a deep lyric earth, rising to the surface of poetry with ease. She speaks in mythical and fabulist associations, in utterances that relish in mystery.

Again and again, we encounter the stone—this most ancient of immutable objects. At times she renders it as a classic metaphor for the void ("I remember you are flintier than a butcher"), but in her glorious lament "My World," the stone becomes a liberating image, a quiet talisman that might promise ceasefire:

> My God, I'm from another world
> Where black hearts are made of stone
> A world that is steady, endlessly monochrome,
> peaceful and serene.

In the hymn of "Human, Stone, Iron," the speaker finds stability in communion with the rock: "Say that behind this rough wall / a woman married stone." The hard elements become her tribe:

> Stone and iron are my family here
> Stone and I have a pact to endure together
> > Let me wander with him on the rocky path of patience.

Another recurring image is the closed or shattered bud, the abandoned container of potential: "Speak of unopened buds / Speak the words sleeping in the heart." I'm compelled to read these lines as an allegory for her own life as a young woman ensnared by the patriarchal culture of Afghanistan, whether with or without the Taliban. The bud, after all, can be hard as a stone—but it also carries within it a hope, or even a rage, to break open into blossom.

This liberation, as per Anjuman's speakers, can be located only in the act of writing itself. In the titular poem of *Gul-e-Dodi*, one of her best and strangest works, the poet's voice rises with the creative power of Promethean fire:

> From this strange seething
> my notebook suddenly
>   comes alive—its papery features
>   blush
> It is a rare flower
> Yet the body
>   gathers its smell and color
>   from these wisps of smoke

Words are not nothing, this speaker declares. Words carry within them the potential to transform reality. Even the paper blushes, as if ashamed. Indeed, in the original Farsi, the word for "my poem" (شعرم, *sher-e-man*) is remarkably close to the word for "shame" (شرم, *sharm*); the translators' work here is commendable for transmuting the wordplay that might otherwise be lost. All of the translations invigorate the poems with the casual elegance of the English language, while retaining their rich multitude and formal experimentation. Every language is equipped with its own ghosts, murmurings of history, etymological shadows, idioms, and music—but it is an astonishing feat that Diana Arterian and Marina Omar have achieved here. Reading the elegiac and feverish poems collected in this book, I am reminded that buds do break open, even when they are carried across borders.

I encountered Anjuman's face in a public place once more, in September of 2019, during my first trip to Kabul, the city my parents had fled a year before I was born. On one of my last days, I visited an orphanage for girls of all ages and ethnicities, founded by a group of activists and philanthropists. The girls received a secular and socialist education, didn't have to wear headscarves, and were encouraged to play instruments, to sing, to dance, to learn martial arts, to paint, and to write poetry. A poem by Pablo Neruda and a mural of Che Guevara graced the walls. And in that hallway of cultural icons hung a large photograph of Nadia Anjuman. She is posing in front of a bookshelf in Iran, where she celebrated her poetry. She is wearing a black dress. Her black hair peeks out from under her black chador—through the trick of light, it almost looks like she isn't covered at all. The expression on her face is still serious, but she doesn't look as melancholy anymore. She is not a cat furled in her professor's office; she is a young woman at the beginning of her career. She is an idol, kin to everyone.

On the day that I am writing this introduction, in 2025, ten years after I read my first Anjuman poem and twenty years after she died, that orphanage does not exist anymore. The girls are scattered across the globe; the lucky ones have become refugees. It has been almost four years since the fall of Kabul, which resulted in a new Taliban regime. Twenty years of war have resulted in nothing, it seems. Afghanistan is currently the only country in the world where girls are not allowed to pursue education beyond sixth grade; they are even banned from dancing and laughing in public. Given this context, it feels redundant to call *Smoke Drifts* an important book. These poems have always been important. Even the Irish poet Eavan Boland wrote about Anjuman's work and life in an essay on national poets, "Without a Country: A Detail," published in *The American*

Poetry Review in 2014. Perhaps Anjuman really can be considered a national poet of Afghanistan. At the very least, she is a poet of a country that cannot be. The page blushes, it burns. And smoke drifts toward the future: it carries the music of the past, a warning, a caress, the scent of sweet basil.

It's a loss for humanity and a loss for poetry that Nadia Anjuman's life was clipped short. And while her poems cannot be extricated from the ruins of her circumstances, for they were born out of them, they also transcend them. Having survived, these poems serve as an anthem for the struggle for liberation that Afghan women have fought for centuries. Afghan women are not voiceless. It is our responsibility, as readers of poetry, as citizens of the earth, to listen to what they say. "I am not that weak willow tree that trembles in the wind," Anjuman wrote. "I am an Afghan girl, and so I howl."

دود می‌آید
نادیا انجمن

Smoke Drifts
Selected Poems

عبث

نیست شوقی که زبان باز کنم از چه بخوانم
من که منفور زمانم چه بخوانم چه نخوانم

چه بگویم سخن از شهد که زهر است به کامم
وای از مشت ستمگر که بکوبیده دهانم

نیست غمخوار مرا در همه دنیا به که نازم
چه بگریم، چه بخندم، چه بمیرم، چه بمانم

من و این کنج اسارت، غم ناکامی و حسرت
که عبث زاده ام مُهر بباید به زبانم

دانم ای دل که بهاران بود و موسم عشرت
منِ پربسته چه سازم که پریدن نتوانم

گرچه دیری‌ست خموشم نرود نغمه ز یادم
زانکه هر لحظه به نجوا سخن از دل برهانم

یاد آن روز گرامی که قفس را بشگافم
سر برون آرم ازین عزلت و مستانه بخوانم

من نه آن بید ضعیفم که ز هر باد بلرزم
دخت افغانم و برجاست که دایم به فغانم

دلو ۱۳۷۸

In Vain

I don't want to open my mouth, what can I sing
I am despised these days—so what if I sing or not

What can I say of honey when it tastes like poison on my tongue
I curse the brutal fist that smashed my mouth

There is no one in the world I can rely on
So what if I cry, I laugh, I die, I linger

Alone in this corner with only defeat and regret
I was born in vain—my tongue is sealed shut

I know it is spring, my heart, a time of celebration
But I am a clipped wing, I can't fly

Though I have been silent for some time, I remember the song
I pull the words from my heart in an endless whisper

Celebrate that day when I will break from this miserable cage
and emerge, drunkenly singing

I am not that weak willow tree that trembles in the wind
I am an Afghan girl, and so I howl

Dalvæ 1378 / Taurus 1999

آسایش

خلوت پاک مرا وسوسه می‌آلاید
چهرهٔ عمر مرا واقعه می‌آلاید
من مگر بستر بگشادهٔ رودم که مدام
بر سرم سیل حوادث پی هم می‌آید
چشم من گر هوس منزل رؤیا بکند
جادهٔ خواب مرا دلهره‌یی پیماید
چه کنم، خانهٔ آرامش غم‌هاست دلم
هرکه زین طایفه ره یافت درآن می‌پاید
می‌دوم من که بیابم ره آرامش چرخ
کینه‌توزانه بر این فاصله می‌افزاید
دیشبم قبربه خواب آمد و آسوده شدم
آدم آنجاست که بی‌دغدغه می‌آساید

حمل ۱۳۸۱

Peace

Temptation mottles my solitude
Disaster mottles the face of my life
Am I an open riverbed
endlessly flooded by the storm of misfortune?
If my eye craves dreams
worry steps into sleep's road
What can I do? My heart is woe's bed
All members of that tribe who find it linger there
I run, searching for a quiet path
but fate hatefully lengthens my way
Last night I dreamed of my grave, and was at peace—
that place where one can rest without dread

Hamal 1381 / Aries 2002

عزت سرخ

...و عاقبت به حضور بهار پی بردیم
به عطر گمشدهٔ روزگار پی بردیم
زمین و هرچه در او هست در ستایش ماست
که ما به معنی فرجام کار پی بردیم
بگو به سنگ نیارد دل از زمانه به تنگ
که ما به ارزش آن انتظار پی بردیم
ز بسکه شستهٔ باران چشم خویش شدیم
به عمق روشنی چشمه‌سار پی بردیم
چو در کنار نشستیم و رنگ هم گشتیم
به راز عزت سرخ انار پی بردیم
دگر به صفحهٔ دل جای گرد نیست که ما
به حسن آیینهٔ بی‌غبار پی بردیم
درخت خاطر ما بیش از این خزان‌زده نیست
که عاقبت به حضور بهار پی بردیم

۱۳۸۱

Red Majesty

...and we realized spring was finally here
We realized the lost scent of life
The earth and everything in it admires us
for we realized the purpose of resolve
Tell the stone not to worry over a moment
for we realized the power of waiting
The streams from our eyes cleansed us endlessly
and we realized the wisdom of the well's light
When we sat nestled side by side, so alike and sure,
we realized the secret of the pomegranate's red majesty
Now dust has no place on our heart's page
for we realized the beauty of a clear mirror
Our mind's tree is no longer devastated by autumn
for we realized spring was finally here

1381 / 2001-2002

تا بی‌کران خالی

آن‌روزها او از خودی لبریز بود
می‌پرورانیدند دستانش
نورستهٔ بی‌ریشه را درخویش
تا بارور گردد

آن‌روزها، در زلال جاری اندیشه‌هایش
پربهایان گونه‌گون بودند
آن‌روزها گاهی
درختان زیر دستش درس می‌خواندند

آن‌روزها اندام‌هایش رام او بودند
شاید از شکوهش می‌هراسیدند

ولی امروز
او دست‌هایش خشک و بی‌بارند
چشم‌هایش سوخته، خالی‌ست
زلال فکر هایش نیز اینک در دل مرداب می‌میرد

به پاها اعتمادش نیست
گویی کج‌روی کردند و با فرمان دیگرها
به راه دیگری رفتند

و او در کنج خاموشی نشسته
رفته تا اعماق دریای فراموشی
و از یاد زمان خالی است
آن
تا بی‌کران خالی است

ثور ۱۳۸۰

Eternal Pit

In the past, she was surrounded by kin
Her hands nurtured
the rootless sprig
        until it bore fruit

In the past, many rare thoughts
        ran in the clear current of her mind
In the past, from time to time,
        her hand trained the trees

In the past, even her limbs were tame,
        perhaps fearing her power

But now
her hands are dry and bare
her eyes burnt sockets
her clear thoughts are dying, buried in a swamp

She distrusts even her feet
They seem to defy her, obey others,
        take her on a different road

She sits in a corner of silence
        lost in a sea's abyss of forgetfulness
        emptied of the thought of time
            That
            is an eternal pit

Sawr 1380 / Taurus 2001

آدم، سنگ، آهن

درین بن‌بست پولادین
تن دیوار را با جسم در پیوند جاویدی‌ست
گسستن را نشاید
آه، دربان!
بس کن، این کوبیدنت با سنگ بی‌هوده است
کلید این‌جاست، اما قفل بر دروازه جوشیده است
برو دربان، برو بگذار گوش مغز من یک دم . . . . بیارامد
من این‌جا با تبار سنگ و آهن سخت خوکردم
مرا با سنگ پیمانی‌ست در هم‌طاقتی
بگذار با او هم‌قدم در سنگلاخ صبر می‌گردم

مرا از زمهریر مرگ باکی نیست
به جانم ضربه‌های دست توفان اتفاق دردناکی نیست
مگو از کیمیای آب‌ها با من
مگو از آبی بی‌انتها با من
که من با آسمان تیرۀ مرداب دل بستم
من این‌جا ریشه دارم
در زمینی آهنین کز ابرهای سربی یک آسمان پولاد توفانی‌ست
مرا کز شاخه‌هایم دم به دم زنجیر می‌روید، ببر از یاد
برو دربان، برو نگذار دستانت ازین پولاد کوبیدن بیازارد
ترا تاب شکستن نیست
من اما خوب می‌دانم که آدم، سنگ، آهن
دست در بازوی هم تا انتهای جاده‌های درد همراهند

Human, Stone, Iron

In this iron corner
the wall's body is forever fixed to the door's flesh
It will never split
Ah, doorkeeper!
Stop—your pounding the stone is useless
The key is here, but the lock is rotted shut
Go away doorkeeper, let my mind's ear
rest . . . . just once
Stone and iron are my family here
Stone and I have a pact to endure together
    Let me wander with him on the rocky path of patience

I am not afraid of the cold hell of death
The storm's blows don't hurt me
Don't talk of water's alchemy
Don't talk of an endless blue
I'm devoted with the dark sky of this swamp
I have taken root here
in an iron land with a leaden sky
                that storms
Forget me—shackles sprout from my branches
Go away doorkeeper, don't hurt yourself pounding on iron
You can't bear it, you'll break
I know all too well that human, iron, and stone
     go hand-in-hand to the end of pain's eternal road
                  strolling together

و از طغیان وحشت‌ها و از جولان ظلمت‌ها
نمی‌کاهند
برو دربان، برو دست تو خالی نیست
برو افسانهٔ سنگین دنیایم به دستانت
برو وین قصه را در شهر سرتاپا حکایت کن
بگو در پشت این دیوار سنگی
دختری با سنگ عقد جاودانی بست
و در اعماق سختی‌ها
به نسل آهنین پیوست

قوس ۱۳۸۰

Their company doesn't stop the riot of fears,
                          the lurking darkness
Go away doorkeeper, go—your hands aren't empty
Go, you hold the heavy story of my world
Go tell it to the city
Say that behind this rough wall
a woman married stone
and in the depths of misery
                      she joined the children of iron

Qaws 1380 / Sagittarius 2001

چگونه

چگونه
از کدام کوچه‌های بی‌خطا
سوار، راه خانه جست‌وجو کند
کجاست کنج آرامشی
که خسته جان لحظه‌ها
دمی به خواب رو کند
زندگی هنوز
هم‌عنان خواب‌های تب‌زده
تازشی شگفت‌گونه بر بساط روح آدم است
چشم بستن و رها شدن زدست دردها
رهسپار وادی خیال
یک دو لحظه بی‌خودی مرگ
وانگهی
پای خسته، خون به لب شکسته، خشک کام
خویش را میان سنگلاخ یافتن
پیش چشم
منظری ز دود و آتش و سراب
در گلو شکستن صدای
آب، آب
ناگهان به ضرب لرزشی غریب و پرتپش
روی بستر عرق شنا
چشم باز کردن و به خویش آمدن

اسد ۱۳۸۲

How

How
should a wandering rider find her way home
Through which precise alleys
Where is the peaceful corner
where one, exhausted by the seconds of life,
can sleep
Leashed to the horse of feverish dreams,
life is a dreadful gallop
charging through the feast of the spirit
You close your eyes and break free from pain's grip
wending your way to the valley of imagination
One or two moments under the spell of death
and then—
tired feet, bloody lips, dry mouth
You find yourself in a rocky place
Before your eyes
only fumes, fire, and mirage
A broken sound in your throat:
> *water, water*

Suddenly, a trembling, something strange and throbbing
Swimming in a bed of sweat
you open your eyes and sober up

Asad 1382 / Leo 2003

انحنا

برای پرورش راست قامتان شعرم
چقدر حوصله سقف‌های شهر
نابلند است

برای قد کشیدن
حتی روزنه‌یی نیست
و اندام‌های شعر من
چه با قناعت
در خمیده‌گی به خواب رفته اند
و هیچ دستی بیدار
هیچ سقفی را
بر انداختنی نیست
کوتاهی اندیشهٔ رسایی را
قیاس نمی‌توان کرد
این‌جا در انحنا باید زیست
در انحنا باید مرد

سنبله ۱۳۸۲

Bent

I want to guide my poems upright
but the reach of the city's ceilings
                is low and arched

There isn't even a crack
                to push through
So, prudently, my poems
have fallen asleep
hunched over
There is no vigilant hand
to break through
                these domes
No one will ever see
                the limits of their thoughts
Here you live bent
and you die bent

Sunbala 1382 / Virgo 2003

یک حکایت

بخت سیمین مرا تا دیدند
چه حسودانه زمن دزدیدند
اسبم از خانه به غارت بردند
و وقیحانه به من تازیدند
وای ازین طایفه رنگ و ریا
که به یک‌رنگی من خندیدند
هرچه در بود به رویم بستند
دشنه بر پنجره‌ها پیچیدند
چشم اگر میل گشودن می‌کرد
میخ آتش‌زده می‌کوبیدند
خون من گاه چو جاری می‌شد
گرگ می‌گشته و می‌نوشیدند
یک بدن بود و هزاران خنجر
رگ رگ جان مرا ببریدند
ازچه ره برقلمم می‌بستند
کج‌روی از قلمم کی دیدند
از چه از باغچهٔ کوچک لب
گل لبخند مرا می‌چیدند
دشمنی ازچه به من می‌کردند
مگر این طایفه گژدم بودند
ازچپاول‌گری احساسم
شاد گردیده وخوش خوابیدند
دود بیداد چنان افزون گشت
کاسمان‌ها عصبی گردیدند
ناگهان رعد به غوغا برخاست
ابرها گریه کنان غریدند

A Story

When they glimpsed my silvery fortune
they stole from me, jealously—
they kidnapped my horse
shamelessly using it to rush at me
Ugh! Curse that gang of cheats and frauds
who mocked my sincerity
They slammed every door in my face
set daggers on every window
When I opened an eye
they hammered in white-hot nails
When I bled
they turned into wolves and drank
Vein by vein they cut at my life,
thousands of blades in my one body
Why shackle my pen—
they never saw it stray
Why clip the budding smile
from the small garden of my lips
Why such hatred
Perhaps they were a nest of scorpions
After ransacking my senses
they slept, satisfied
The skies grew fitful
with the fumes of my torment
Thunder boomed
and the clouds roared,

برقی از سینه به بیرون دادند
که ستون‌های زمین لرزیدند
«قوم» وحشت‌زده بیدارشدند
و سرآسیمه به خود خشکیدند
چاردیوار فروریخت به خاک
چشم‌ها عقده‌گشا باریدند
آخرین لحظهٔ امید مرا
ابرها عمر نوین بخشیدند
این منم! من که سخن می‌گویم
کاش بودند و مرا می‌دیدند

حوت ۱۳۸۰

their chests burst with lightning
The pillars of the earth shook
and the clan woke up in a panic
They darted around—then froze, stunned
Their four walls collapsed
My eyes rained tears of resolve
At my hope's dying breath,
the clouds gave it life
This is I! She who speaks
If only those thieves could see me now

Hoot 1380 / Pisces 2002

باغ من

دوســت دارم معنی امید را باور کنم
راه غــم بر بندم و فکر ره دیگر کنم

ریشــه‌های زنده‌گی را آب‌یاری لازم است
بعد ازین آینده را نوشــاب در ساغر کنم

چشــمۀ مهتاب را در سایه‌ها جاری کنم
ســرو ها و سبزه‌ها را سبز در اختر کنم

باغ من در روشــنی رشک گهرها می‌شود
گر گل خورشــید را دعوت به این محشر کنم

روزگار از کار من افســانه‌ها خواهد نوشت
دوســت دارم سینۀ تاریخ را پر زر کنم

انجمن گر در ســرودن‌ها مرا یاری کند
شــعر ناب خویش را آذین هر دفتر کنم

جدی ۱۳۷۹

My Garden

I will believe in the meaning of hope
I will shut the door on grief and find another way

The roots of life need sustenance
So I will raise my glass to the future

I will let moonlight's spring flow through shadows
I will grow cypress trees even in the stars

If I invite orange lilies to this affair
I will make gems envy my radiant garden

In time my work will be legendary
I will fill the chest of history with gold

If Anjuman helps me write these verses
I will gild every book with pure poetry

Jaddi 1379 / Capricorn 2000

حقیقت را پذیرا باش

چرا دربند رؤیایی؟
تو ای آشفتهٔ مبهوت و سرگردان!
ای انسان
که نامت اشرف مخلوق یزدان است و
احوالت به سامان است
من و تو چون خسی بر روی دریاییم
نمی‌دانیم تا یک لحظهٔ دیگر
باد وهم‌انگیز ما را سوی ساحل می‌کشاند
یا به توفان بلامان می‌سپارد درتباهی‌ها
من و تو برگ پائیزیم و دست خشمگین باد
ما را می‌تواند سرنگون سازد

تو ای یک‌دانه دختر
ای پریشان‌موی زیباروی
که با نیم نگاهت عالمی را زیر و رو سازی
وزلفانت چو زنجیر بلا صد دل به دام آرد
چه سود از این همه طنازی و دل‌سوختن، چون فتنه‌انگیزان
به خود گویی:
«جهان از من
زمین و آسمان از من
بهاران با فضای عطرآمیزش
چمن با شاخه‌های سبزگل‌ریزش...»
نمی‌دانی که تا سر بر کنی، چون گل
به چنگال زمان پژمرده می‌گردی؟
دل آزردهٔ دلداده را نشکن
که حُسنت جاودانی نیست،
و دست سرد پائیزت بلرزاند

Accept the Truth

Why cage yourself in fantasy?
You dazed and troubled drifter
Oh Humanity,
the noblest of God's creations
with easy lives
We are driftwood bobbing on the sea
At any moment
an awful gale might send us to shore
                     or give us to the storm of disaster and ruin
We are the autumn leaf—wind's furious hand
                     might hurl us downward
You rare girl
a beauty with strewn hair
who can upend the world with a sidelong glance
       Your eyelashes can shackle a hundred hearts into a chain of ruin
What good is all this rebellious flirtation and heartbreak?
You tell yourself:
         The world is mine
            The sky and earth
            The spring with its sweet air
            The garden with its blossoming green branches...
Don't you realize when you raise your head, like a flower
                     you will wither in the claws of time?
Don't break the aching heart of a lover
your beauty won't last forever
               Autumn's cold grip will shake you

چرا بی‌هوده مغروری؟
من و تو شمع سوزانیم و همچون مرغ بسمل جان به لب داریم
حقیقت را پذیرا باش
تو ای سوداگر بهروز و ثروت‌مند
که ازسر تا به پا غرق تجمل‌های دنیایی
سرت را در گریبان کن
پریشان مادرت رنجور و بیمارست -
و تو غافل شراب حرص می‌نوشی
چه سود از سیم و زر اندوختن،
ایام و شب‌هایت به ترس اندر
که شاید دست تقدیرت بگیرد آن‌همه عز و جلال و حشمت و مکنت
چرا از حق گریزانی؟
مگر آخر کجا باید شدن
ای راه بی‌منزل
اگر روزی خبر یابی که مادر ترک دنیا کرد
چه خواهی کرد اگر خورشید گردون را به‌دست آری؟
گمان کن گنج قارون، قدرت نمرودیان از توست
بپرس از خویش:
آیا می‌توانی لحظهٔ کوتاه را از آن خود سازی؟
و یا با مختصر بیمار تب‌داری در آمیزی؟
ندانستم چه می‌خواهی
من و تو سایهٔ ابریم
من و تو جرقهٔ خاموش و راه بی‌سرانجامیم
ندانستی چرا هستیم و
راز خلقت ما چیست؟
زمان یک لحظهٔ کوتاه هم در قدرت ما نیست
تو ای ارباب قانون ای تو در اوج توانایی
گرانسانی و خوی آدمی داری

Why so arrogant?
We are like a burning candle—like a wounded bird, our souls leaving
    our lips
Accept the truth
You rich and lucky merchant
steeped in the world's comforts from head to toe
Look inward
While you drink the wine of greed with relish
              your anxious mother is ill and suffering
What good is hoarding gold and silver?
Your days and nights are awash with the fear
that the hand of fate might take all your glory and grandeur and wealth
Why run from the truth?
Where will you go—there is no place to rest
              on that road
If one day you find your mother has died—
              what could you do, even if you could hold the sun?
Imagine Korah's wealth and Nimrod's power were yours
Ask yourself:
Can you hold a moment?
Or even comfort a feverish patient?
I don't know what you want
We are a cloud's shadow
We are a snuffed spark, the dead end of an alley
Don't you know why we exist,
        the secret of our making?
           Every moment, we are powerless to time
Oh, master of laws, you apex of strength!

گره بگشای از کار نگون‌بختی
پناه بی‌پناهان باش و حاتم‌وار
دست ناتوانان گیر
ایا انسان
چرا لبریز حرمان و تمنایی
چرا دربند پستی‌های دنیایی
تو در اندوه بی‌جایی
تو تنهایی و دستانت تهی از یار همراهی
ترا ره توشه‌یی باید که راهی می‌شوی آخر
نشاید سیم و زر بردن به عقبا، فکر دیگر کن
خیال‌اندوزی از ما نیست
باید واقف از احوال خود باشیم
حقیقت را پذیرا باش و
رؤیا را ز سر در کن

عقرب ۱۳۷٦

If you are human and decent

unravel the knot of misery

Become a refuge for the homeless and, like Haatam,

        hold the hands of the weak

Humanity,

why are you brimming with privation and desire

Why are you caged by material vices

You bear the grief of eviction

You are lonely, your hand without a friend's grip

You will have to leave your hoarded possessions in the end

You can't take gold and silver to the next world—think

We can't daydream

We must know our fate

Accept the truth

        and force that dream from your head

Aqrab 1376 / Scorpio 1997

نورسته‌ها

ای خاك!
ای خواب رفته بی‌خبر از حادثات مرگ
در انتهای باور یك رؤیا
از خویش مطمئن

بر اعتماد نازك نورسته‌ها
درون تو
چندین گروه مكر
چاقو به مشت و آب به دست اند.
بیدار شو ببین كه چگونه
این جلوه می‌دهند و از آن كار می‌برند
تا از خدا نپرسی دیگر
نورسته‌های سبز چرا زرد میشوند.

اسد ۱۳۸۰

Fresh Buds

Oh, Earth
drowsy and ignorant of death
caught in a waning dream
self-assured

The brittle trust of fresh buds abused
    by the many crafty gangs
    you carry—
        their fisted knives hidden, hands outstretched with water
Wake up—
see how these men show one hand then use the other
    Don't ask God again
        why your fresh green buds only yellow and fade

Asad 1380 / Leo 2001

زهرآگین

آن شب...
در محفل خصوصی گژدم‌ها
یک بحث داغ و تلخ
دیری ادامه یافت
موضوع: »زرق زهر به اندام‌های علم!«
در انتخاب سم
سامان نمی‌گرفت و به مطلب نمی‌رسید
ناگاه از آن میان
یک تن که بود زشت‌تر از اصل نسل خویش
چون تیغ برگشاد زبان
گفت این‌چنین
شب در گذشتن است و مجال درنگ نیست
تا چشم‌های طعمه به خواب اند
خیزید و نیش‌گاه بجویید
میراث مانده بر من
یک شیشه از هلاهل چندین هزار سالۀ جدم
ایثارگر منم...

سرطان ۱۳۸۰

Poison

That night…
the scorpions gathered in secret
A fierce argument
    went on for hours
The subject: *injecting poison into bodies of knowledge!*
Yet they couldn't reach a verdict
    on which poison to use
Suddenly, in the group
the ugliest of them all
loosed his tongue like a sword
    and said:
        The night is passing—there's no time to waste
While our prey have their eyes closed,
rise and find a point to sting
I have inherited
an ancient jar of deadly venom from my ancestors
Now I am the generous one who will pass it on…

    Sarataan 1380 / Cancer 2001

جهان من

جای من این‌جا نیست
من زجای دگرم
به‌خدا من ز جهان دگرم
ز جهانی که در آن قلب سیاه از سنگ است
ز جهانی که سراپا همه جا یک‌رنگ است
همه جا صلح و صفاست
و نیاموزد گرگ
درس بی‌دادگری انسان را

تا کسی با تیری
نشکند بال و پر مرغان را
ز جهانی که منم
هیچ‌کس بی‌خود و مست از می قدرت‌ها نیست
وکسی حسرت آرامش زندان نخورد
بحث پیرامن افزایش ثروت‌ها نیست
وکسی تاج طلایی به کسی نفروشد
کس عزادار مروت‌ها نیست
ودل از سردی دستانی کسی یخ نزند
ز جهانی که منم
علمش لوحه‌یی از باغ بهشت است و علم‌دارانش
مردمی پاک‌دل اند
لحظه‌هایش همه شادی بخشند
و دمی نیست که چشمان کسی
خالی از نور امیدی باشد
وشبی نیست که لب‌های کسی
خالی از بیت سرودی باشد
عاقبت خواهم رفت

My World

I don't belong here
I come from somewhere else
My God, I'm from another world
Where black hearts are made of stone
A world that is steady, endlessly monochrome,
peaceful and serene
Where wolves don't learn lessons of cruelty
                from humanity,
and no one with arrows
snaps the wings of birds
In my world
no one is blind-drunk on power
No one longs for the peace of prison
Talk doesn't circle around getting rich
and no one peddles golden crowns
No one mourns compassion
and a hand's chill doesn't freeze the heart
In my world
the flag is from paradise, and its bearers
                have pure hearts
Every moment in my world is joyful
and a person's eye is never
                without hope's spark
There is never a night when a person's lips
      don't carry a song
Someday I will go

به جهانی که در آن دست تمدن نرسیده است هنوز
و سراپا همه جا زیبایی است
و تو ای آنکه ترا قدرت درک سخن است
کاش همگام من و همسفر من باشی
من وت و باهم ازین غمکده بیرون برویم
به جهانی که سزاوار من و توست
برای من و تو
و سراپا همه جا زیبایی‌ست
به جهانی که خیالش از دور
مثل دیدار خدا رؤیائی‌ست

جدی ۱۳۷۹

to the world untouched by civilization
and there is beauty everywhere
And you, the one who understands—
I wish you would come with me
You and I will leave this dreary place
and go to a world that is worthy of us
    For you and me,
        there is beauty everywhere
        in a world—its distant vision
        like seeing God in a dream

Jaddi 1379 / Capricorn 2000

برو

گذشتم از تو اگر جان وگر جهان بودی
نخواهمت دگر ای صبح نو دمیده برو
برو که بار دگر همتبار شب باشم
که تار و پود من و شب بههم تنیده، برو
برو که خسته ام از قیل و قال وصل و فراق
ازین منازعه جانم به لب رسیده برو
مگو مگو که امید است بر طلوع دگر
مرا که عمر امیدم به سر رسیده برو
من از دیار غممم، با تو کی درآمیزم
حدیث درد منِ زار ناشنیده برو
مرا به خلوت زندان دردها بگذار
تو ای پرندۀ شاد قفس ندیده برو

ثور ۱۳۷۹

Go

I will walk past you even if you are my soul, the world
Bright new morning, I'm done with you—go
Go so I can return to the night, my family
Night's threaded texture and mine are woven together—go
Go, for I'm tired of the battle of our linking and pulling apart
The struggle is killing me, go
Don't—don't say there is hope for another dawn
My hope is nearly dead, go
I'm from the land of grief—how can I relate to you
Don't listen to the story of my pain, go
Just leave me alone in my pain's deserted prison
Happy bird who has never seen a cage, go

Sawr 1379 / Taurus 2000

کوه دریا

ایا تبعیدیان کوه گمنامی
ای گوهران نام‌هاتان خفته در شــن‌زار خاموشی
ای محو گشته یادهاتان
یادهای آبی روشن
به ذهن موج گل‌آلود دریای فراموشــی

زلال جاری اندیشه‌هاتان کو؟
کدامین دســت غارت‌گر به یغما برد
تندیس طلای ناب رؤیاتان
درین توفان ظلمت‌زا
کجا شــد زورق سیمین آرامش نشان ماه پیماتان؟

پس ازین زمهریر مرگ‌زا
دریا اگر آرام گیرد
ابــر اگر خالی کند از عقده‌ها دل
دختر مهتاب اگر مهر آورد
لب‌خند بخشد

کوه اگر دل نرم ســازد سبزه آرد
بارور گردد
یکــی از نام‌هاتان بر فراز قله‌ها
خورشید خواهد شد؟
طلوع یادهاتان
یادهای آبی روشن
به چشــم ماهیان خسته از سیلاب و

Mountain, Sea

Oh, exiles on the mountain of oblivion,
the glittering gems of your names are asleep in mute sand
Your dim memories
      those bright blue memories
      are caught under a wave in the mind's muddied sea of amnesia

Where is your shining wit?
Which hand looted the rare
              golden effigy of your dreams?
Where did your calm silvery moon-bound ship go
in this dark storm?

If the sea quiets
      after this deadly frozen hell
If the cloudburst relaxes
If the moon's daughter brings feeling
         and laughter

If the mountain's heart softens and greens,
         grows fertile—
then will your names be the sun
        at its peaks?
Will the dawn of your memories
those bright blue memories
become a flash of hope

از باران ظلمت‌ها هراسان
جلوهٔ امید خواهد شد؟
آیا تبعیدیان کوه گمنامی!

قوس ۱۳۸۰

in the tired eyes of the storm-born fish
afraid of the raining darkness?
Oh, exiles on the mountain of oblivion!

Qaws 1380 / Sagittarius 2001

سر بکش! سر بکش!

قصهٔ درد دل شنیدن چیست؟
شرح سوزان داغ دیدن چیست؟

یار گر رفت حق به همراهش
در غمش پیرهن دریدن چیست؟

جاده بی‌آخرست هان! مشتاب
سوی بی‌انتها دویدن چیست؟

رشته با هر چه هست می‌بندم
از زمین و زمان بریدن چیست

او اگر دوست نیست من هستم
دست از دوستی کشیدن چیست؟

حتماً از بهر حاجتی صیاد
پی صیدم بود رمیدن چیست؟

در قفس نیز می‌شود خوش خواند
در سر اندیشهٔ پریدن چیست؟

راست از در درآ، سلامی کن
دیگر از کنج پرده دیدن چیست؟

جام او و هر چه هست نوشین است
سربکش! سربکش! چشیدن چیست؟

Drink! Drink!

Why listen to the heart's complaints?
Or the burning portrait of grief's pain?

If your lover leaves, may God be with him
Why tear your clothes at the loss?

Don't rush—this road is endless!
Why gallop toward infinity?

I tie myself to everything
Why cut yourself from the earth and sky?

If your lover is gone, I am here
Why break all bonds?

Surely the hunter has set his mark for a reason
Why run away? He must hound me

You can sing with grace from a cage
Why cling to the memory of flight?

Come through the door and say hello
Why peer sideways from behind a curtain?

Whatever his cup holds, it's sweet
Why only sip? Drink! Drink!

می‌رسیم عاقبت به نخل‌آباد
صحبت تلخ نارسیدن چیست؟

قوس ۱۳۸۰

We will reach the palm grove eventually
Why the bitter talk of never arriving?

Qaws 1380 / Sagittarius 2001

زندان

درین سرای سکوت
یکی نمانده که دل خو کند به آوازش
زباغ سوخته‌اش بوی دود می‌آید
و سروهای رسایش در انتظار زلزله اند
که سر به خاک نهند
دریغ از آن که به پایان رسیده آغازش

هر آن‌که بال و پری دارد و توانایی
به‌سان تیر ازین بی‌نشان گریزان است
به وقت بال‌گشایی و لحظه‌های فرار

خوش است حالت شوق عجیب پروازش
و آنکه قوت پرواز خود نمی‌بیند
فتاده گوشه‌یی ویرانه در پریشانی
کجاست یار سخن‌ساز و قصه‌پردازش
در این سرای سکوت
امیدها همه در انتظار می‌میرند
نهال‌ها همه در نوبهار می‌میرند
به هرکه می‌نگری
به خود شکسته ز تکرار روزها سیر است
طلوع نیز ازین بخت تیره دلگیر است

ازین سرای خموشان و بی‌سرانجامان
فرار باید کرد
به سوی شهر افق‌های دور و ناپیدا
به هر کجا که هیاهوی زیستن باشد

Prison

In this house of silence
there is no one left—the heart gets used to its song
The smell of smoke drifts from her burnt garden
where her grand cypresses wait for the earthquake
that will bring their heads to earth
How tragic that her beginning has come to an end

Anyone who has feathers and the strength
flees in an instant—she spreads her wings
and shoots from this nameless place like a bullet

The rare thrill of her flight is satisfying
She who doesn't find the strength to fly
suffers, prone, in a corner of ruins
Where did the friend who told her stories go?
In this house of silence
hopes die from waiting
saplings die even in spring
In every face you see
a person, broken, fed up with the tedium of days
Even the sunrise is solemn with its dark fate

You have to escape
from this cursed house of silence
to a city of far and invisible horizons
where there is the clamor of life

اگر که بال نباشد
به پای باید رفت
و پا اگر نبود دست دل به دریا زد
به آب باید زد
ز باد باید خواست
زهر رهی که میسر بود ازین زندان
فرار باید کرد
فرار باید کرد

دلو ۱۳۷۹

If you have no wings

go on foot

If you have no legs, leap into the dark

You must plunge into the sea

You must ask the wind

On any path that can lead away from this prison

you have to escape

you have to escape

Dalvæ 1379 / Aquarius 2001

دل دیوانه

نه سیر باغ وگلزار و نه آب ودانه می‌خواهم
من آن مرغم که تنها گوشهٔ ویرانه می‌خواهم
دلی دارم که لبریز است از سودای حسرت‌ها
به این سودایی دل کنج حسرت‌خانه می‌خواهم
ندیدم الفتی از آشنا و یار و دلداری
دلی دردآشنا را با جهان بیگانه می‌خواهم
میان بزم گیتی سوختم در داغ تنهایی
ز درگاه خدای انجمن پروانه می‌خواهم
من از سودای هشیاری ندیدم سود و مقصودی
به استقبال مستی می‌روم، پیمانه می‌خواهم
نمی‌خواهم متاع عقل، مفتون جنونم من
دل دیوانه می‌خواهم، دلی دیوانه می‌خواهم

سنبله ۱۳۷۸

Crazy Heart

I don't want a view of the garden or water or seeds
I am a bird that wants only a corner of ruins
My heart overflows with lost hopes
I want a nook in the house of regret for this heart
I see no kindness from acquaintance, friend, or lover
I want my grieving heart apart from the world
In humanity's feast, the scorch of loneliness branded me
I want a moth from Anjuman's God
No good comes with reason
I want wine, I welcome drunkenness
I don't want intellect, I am drawn to madness
I want a crazy heart, I want a crazy heart

Sunbula 1378 / Virgo 1999

بازیچه

ای جعبهٔ خالی از عروسک
ای هستهٔ خود ز دست داده
ای پا و سرت دریده، خسته
درکنج زباله‌دان فتاده

دیروز ترا به ناز بسیار
بنشسته به تخت طاق دیدم
اندام ترا درست و کامل
زیبندهٔ یک اطاق دیدم

آن پیکر کاغذین و رنگین
همشانهٔ جام‌های زر بود
چشمان نیازمند طفلان
بر قامت تو نظاره‌گر بود

یک‌باره تنت به دست تقدیر
از اوج روانه شد به پستی
من شاهد ماجرات بودم
دیدم که به سادگی شکستی

جسمی که درون پیکرت بود
با هرکه رسید دلبری کرد
بی‌خود شده با تماس هر دست
خندیده و خوش سخنوری کرد

Playthings

Oh, empty box
you've lost your core
The doll you held is torn and ratty
tossed to the edge of the trash heap

Yesterday you were up on the shelf
I saw you, smug
your form whole
I saw you brighten the room

That papery, colorful box
next to gold cups
The groping eyes of children
gazed at your figure

Then your body was in fate's hands
You dropped from that height
I saw your story
I saw how easily you broke

The figure inside you
charmed and flirted with anyone who passed
She laughed and chatted
intoxicated by the touch of hands

با عشوه و ناز سرخوشانه
هوش از سرکوبکان بدر برد
هم هستی خویش را تبه کرد
هم روح ترا به نیستی برد

آن جسم لطیف و نرم و زیبا
از حجرهٔ خویش تا برون شد
یک‌دم به میان خاک غلتید
یک لحظه به چاه سرنگون شد

نه دست و نه پای دارد اکنون
نه تاج و نه موی چنگ در چنگ
بر قامت او اثر نمانده
زان جامهٔ لاله‌ای خوش‌رنگ

در کشمکش میان طفلان
سر از تن او جدا فتاده
لیکن به لبش هنوز باقی‌ست
آن خندهٔ دلنشین ساده

جز پوچی و پایمال گشتن
فرجام چه شد تو را و او را؟
آخر به زباله‌ها سپردند
تندیس قشنگ آرزو را

اینک تو و پیکر شکسته
اینک تو و دست‌های خالی
بازیگر هرزهٔ زمانه
کی می‌شنود اگر بنالی؟

Flirty and pleased
her body stole sense from children
She ruined her life
and destroyed your spirit

That beautiful, soft, smooth body
as she emerged from her box
was suddenly rolling in the dirt—
then down a well in a second

Now she has no hands or feet
no crown or locks of hair
There is not a shred
of her bright tulip-red clothes

In the children's tussle
her head broke off—
but her lips still hold
that charming, simple smile

Aside from being emptied and trampled
what became of you two?
In the end they threw her away—
that beautiful statue of desire

Now you are this broken form
Now you are these empty hands
You are merely time's harlot puppet
Who will care to hear you whimper?

ای جعبهٔ خالی از عروسك
من نیز تهی تر از تو هستم
بازیچه شدم به دست تقدیر
نا چیز شدم، بههم شکستم

دل از بر من جدا فتاده
افسرده و چاك خورده، خونین
پامال جفای دهر گشته
آن گنج گهرنشان رنگین

بازیچه شدن حدیث تلخیست
جز محنت و درد سر ندارد
دستی که من و تو را تبه کرد
از نالهٔ ما حذر ندارد

ای جعبهٔ خالی از عروسك
ای هستئ خود ز دست داده
ای پا و سرت دریده، خسته
در کنج زبالهدان فتاده

ثور ۱۳۸۱

Oh, empty box
I too am empty—even more than you are
I became a plaything in the hands of fate
I became nothing, I broke

My heart has fallen from me
withered, torn, and bloody—
my colorful treasure
trampled by the cruelty of time

To become a plaything is a bitter tale
It only brings trouble and misery
The hand that destroyed us
doesn't hear our whimpers

Oh, empty box
you've lost your core
The doll you held is torn and ratty
tossed to the edge of the trash heap

Sawr 1381 / Taurus 2002

قصه‌های تلخ

ای قصه‌های تلخ
عمری‌ست دفتر دل ما خانهٔ شماست
این چشم‌های غمزده، وین گونه‌های زرد
آثار شوم عادت خصمانهٔ شماست
ای شاخه‌های غم!
صد نوبهار آمد و صد مهرگان گذشت
بس غنچه‌ها که داغ به دل از جهان گذشت
صد راهِ بسته وا شد و صد کاروان گذشت
فرعون مرد و قصهٔ نمرودیان گذشت
اما شما هنوز چنان سبز و تازه اید
گویی ز بطن باغچه امروز زاده اید

ای شعله‌های یأس
یک روز از دیار دل ما سفر کنید
تنها نه قلب ماست سزاوار سوختن
یک بار هم به خانهٔ دیگر گذر کنید

ای قصه‌های تلخ
جان‌ها به لب رسیده ز مهمانی شما
زنهار، جست‌وجوگر مسکن اگر نه اید
فرداست کز خرابهٔ غم‌بار روزگار
ما رخت بسته ایم و شما زار و بی‌پناه
در برزخ زمان
بی‌خانه مانده اید

حمل ۱۳۸۰

Bitter Stories

Bitter stories,
you have made homes of our hearts for a lifetime
These sorrowful eyes, these sallow cheeks
are the grim marks of your presence
Branches of sorrow,
a hundred springs come and a hundred autumns go
buds wither with scorched hearts
a hundred blockades clear and a hundred caravans pass
Pharaoh dies and Nimrod's tale ends
yet you are still green and fresh
as if just sprouted from the dirt

Flames of despair,
leave the reaches of our hearts—
they are not the only things that deserve to burn
For once, pass through another house

Bitter stories,
we are exhausted by your company
If you do not find a new house, beware
Tomorrow we will go from the sorrowful ruins of life
while you, wretched and exposed,
will be left without a home
        in the limbo of time

Hamal 1380 / Aries 2001

شب شعر

شب است و شعر می‌زند شرر به لحظه‌های من
و شوق شانه می‌کند به رشتهٔ صدای من

چه آتش است وای عجب که آب می‌دهد مرا
و عطر روح می‌دمد به پیکر هوای من

ندانم از کدام کوه، کدام کوه آرزو
نسیم تازه می‌وزد به فصل انتهای من

ز ابر نور می‌رسد چنان زلال روشنی
که نیست حاجتی دگر به اشک و های‌های من

جرقه‌های آه من ستاره‌ریز می‌شوند
به عرش لانه می‌کند کبوتر دعای من

سرشک بی‌خودانه‌ام به خط خط کتاب او
نگاه کن چه بی‌بهانه می‌چکد خدای من

زحرف حرف دفتری، ز واژه واژه محشری
قیامتی دمیده از سکوت دیرپای من

سحر مدر حریر وهمی مرا که خوش‌ترم
به شب که شعر می‌زند شرر به لحظه‌های من

عقرب ۱۳۸۱

The Night of Poetry

It is night and poetry ignites my moments
Fervor combs my voice like knotted hair

What kind of fire quenches my thirst
What soulful aroma stirs my air

I don't know from which mountain, which mountain of desire
blows this fresh breeze through my hot solstice

Such pure light falls from a bright cloud
that there is no need for me to weep and wail

Sparks pour out from my sighs like stars
The pigeon of my prayer nestles in the heavens

My wild tears fall, drop after drop, on each line of this book
My God, look how needlessly they flow

Sound to sound, then word to word, then volumes—a riot
Resurrection emerges from my lingering silence

Morning, don't tear at the silk of my illusion
I swear to the night, when poetry ignites my moments

Aqrab 1381 / Scorpio 2002

خورشید دانائی

لب از خاموش بودن می‌گریزد
تن از غم‌پوش بودن می‌گریزد
بیا لب از خموشی باز داریم
دمار از روزگار غم برآریم
لباس از رنگ شادی‌ها بپوشیم
شراب ازجام آزادی بنوشیم
اگر دست زمان اهریمنی کرد
سپاه جهل بر ما دشمنی کرد
اگر بیگانه خصم معرفت نیست
خموشی بیش ازین در مصلحت نیست
زبان از کام ناکامی برون آر
دل از تبعید گمنامی برون آر
بگو ازغنچه‌های ناشگفته
سخن‌های درون سینه خفته
لیاقت‌هایی در زنجیر مانده
سعادت‌هایی در ظلمت نشانده
کنون خورشید دانایی دمیدست
بشارت از خدا بر ما رسیدست
هراس از تیرگی در دل نیاریم
به‌راه حق‌شناسی پا گذاریم

عقرب ۱۳۸۰

The Sun of Knowledge

Lips gallop away from muteness
The body gallops away from grief
Let's avoid silence
Let's raze the realm of sorrow
Let's wear fabric woven with joy
Let's drink wine from freedom's cup
If the hand of fate becomes our enemy
If the army of ignorance becomes our enemy
If wisdom's foe is no longer a stranger
we can't stay silent
Bring the tongue from failure's mouth and use it
Bring the heart from nameless exile
Speak of unopened buds
Speak the words sleeping in the heart
the shackled talents
the joys pushed into darkness
The sun of knowledge is rising
God delivers good news
Let's stop darkness from sowing fear in our hearts
Let's step on the path of honesty

Aqrab 1380 / Scorpio 2001

طعم غزل

یک سبد دلهرهٔ شیرین
آه! فقط
یک سبد دلهرهٔ شیرین
کافی‌ست که در فرداها
هستی کوچک من دیگر بار
در فضای غزلستان تبسم‌ها
آغاز شود
تا دلم باز شود

وای از حجم هجوم تلخی
باز هم زیر درختان حوادث خفتم
در کنارم سبدی لبریز است
و هنوز
هر که از طعم غزل‌های من آگاه شود
چهره در هم آرد

۱۳۸۱

A Taste of Ghazal

One basket, sweet worry
Ah! Just
one basket, sweet worry
One is enough, so that tomorrow
my small life is once again
in the land of ghazals
                      where smiles emerge
                        and my heart opens

Ugh, such an attack of misery
I slept under the tree of disaster again
So beside me a basket overflows with doubt
And yet
anyone who knows the taste of my ghazals
                                  will furrow their brow

1381 / 2001-2002

رشته‌های پولادین

ز بسکه رانده شد از جام لب ترانهٔ من
شکست زمزمه در روح شاعرانهٔ من

مجوی در سخنم معنی نشاط و سرور
که مُرد در تب غم طبع شادمانهٔ من

به چشم دفتر من گر ستاره می‌خوانی
فسانه‌یی‌ست ز رؤیای بی‌کرانهٔ من

مپرس عشق که الهام‌بخش چامهٔ توست
به یاد مرگ بود حرف عاشقانهٔ من

به پای گلبن امید رود خواهم گشت
که کارساز نشد اشک دانه دانهٔ من

اگر چه دختر شهر قصیده و غزلم
خراب و خام بود شعر ناشیانهٔ من

نهال خودسر من دست باغبان نشناخت
مخواه جلوهٔ بسیار از جوانهٔ من

به دست و پا و زبان رشته‌های پولادین
به روی لوح زمان این بود نشانهٔ من

عقرب ۱۳۸۰

Steel Strings

Over and over they pulled the lyric's cup from my lips
finally breaking the humming in my poetic spirit

Don't look for happiness and joy in my words
The fever of sadness killed my joy

If you find stars in my notebook's eye
it is only the myth of my boundless fantasy

Don't ask if love is my pen's muse
I sing my tender words only for death

I will become a river for the roots of hope's rosebush—
my teardrops alone aren't enough

Though I am daughter to the city of elegy and ghazals
my clumsy poem is botched and crude

My wild sprig doesn't know the gardener's hand
Don't expect much beauty from my flowers

Steel strings bind my hands, feet, tongue
so this is my mark on the book of time

Sarataan 1380 / Cancer 2001

گل دودی

من از احساس تهی بودن لب‌ریزم
لبریز
و این فراوانی قحطی‌ست که گهگاه مرا
در تب آتشی مزرعهٔ جانم
می‌جوشاند
و ازین جوشش بی‌آب عجیب
چهرهٔ کاغذی دفتر شعرم، ناگه
جان می‌گیرد
گل می‌اندازد
گل بی‌مانندی‌ست
ولی افسوس تنش را
رگه‌هایی از دود
رنگ و بو می‌بخشند

جدی ۱۳۸۱

Flower of Smoke

I am filled with emptiness
      Filled
With this abundance of want
the field of my being often burns
           simmering with fiery fever
From this strange seething
my notebook suddenly
      comes alive—its papery features
          blush
It is a rare flower
Yet the body
      gathers its smell and color
      from these wisps of smoke

Jaddi 1381 / Capricorn 2003

استغاثه

ای آسمان ببار که این خاک سوخته
در اشتیاق قطرهٔ باران زنده‌گی‌ست
لب‌های خشک و سینهٔ آتش گرفته اش
تصویری از نمایش پایان زنده‌گی‌ست

ای ابر جنبشی که درین سرزمین داغ
چشم هزار مزرعه در انتظار توست
باز آ که کوه‌های زمرد نشان شهر
عمری‌ست جامه کرده سیه سوگوار توست

ای آب ای طبیب طبیعت عیادتی
کز درد دوریت دل گل‌ها شکسته است
دیگر نمانده تاب تحمل به غنچه‌ها
در حسرت تو خنده به لب‌ها شکسته است

یارب روا مدار که دهقان ناتوان
در کورهٔ زمانه لبِ تشنه جان دهد
یک قطره آب رحمت بی‌انتهای تو
بر دست‌های خستهٔ دهقان توان دهد

یارب به کوچیان دل‌افسرده الفتی
یارب به سوز سینه دریا عنایتی
یارب به خشکی لب سوزان چشمه‌ها
بر دشت‌های سوخته، باران رحمتی

Plea

Sky, pour down—this scorched earth aches
for a drop of life's rain
Its lips are dry, its heart on fire,
a portrait of death

Cloud, drift toward this hot land
A thousand fields watch for you
Come back, for the emerald mountains of the city
have worn mourner's clothes for ages

Water, nature's healer, visit us
Your painful absence leaves the flowers heartbroken
The buds have no strength left
Smiles split from lips as they yearn for you

God, don't let the weak farmer
die thirsting in the furnace of time
One drop of your infinite kindness
can revive their tired hands

God, show pity to the grim wanderers
God, show kindness to the burning heart of the sea
God, rain blessings on the creek's baking lips—
on the scorched plateau

ما بندگان نادم و بشکسته قامتیم
غرق گناه گشته و در جهل و ظلمتیم
یارب روا مدار که بیچاره‌تر شویم
برما ببخش گرچه سزاوار محنتیم

آبی بریز بر سر ما کاندر آتشیم
آبی که چشم چشمهٔ خشکیده تر شود
این خاک داغ خوابگه عاشقان توست
هرگز روا مدار که زیر و زبر شود

اسد ۱۳۷۹

We are your subjects, ashamed and broken
drowned in sin, ignorant in darkness
God, don't let us grow more pathetic
Though we deserve to suffer, forgive us

Pour cool water on us—we are in flames
Some water to wet the creek's arid eye
This hot earth is your lover's bed
don't let it churn into total chaos

Asad 1379 / Leo 2000

کاش می‌شد

کاش می‌شد از شراب حسن او سیراب گشتن
یا به عشقش سوختن، یا بر دلش ارباب گشتن
کاش می‌شد اشک بودن، برگل رویش شگفتن
یا که مشک عنبرین زلف او را تاب گشتن
کاش می‌شد گرد بودن، بر سر راهش نشستن
زیر خورشید نگاهش قطره قطره آب گشتن
کاش می‌شد راز بودن، در نگاهش جلوه کردن
برلبان خامش او، واژه‌های ناب گشتن
کاش می‌شد سایه‌گونه هرنفس با دوست بودن
یا شب از شوق حضورش، تا سحر بی‌خواب گشتن
سر به راه دل سپردن، از جدایی‌ها گسستن
در به روی غصه بستن، پا و سر مهتاب گشتن

سرطان ۱۳۷۸

I Wish

I wish I were drunk on the wine of his beauty
or consumed by his love, or living as the master of his heart
I wish I were a teardrop on the flower of his face
or a curl of his perfumed hair
I wish I were the dust sitting in his path
Or melting bit by bit under the sun of his gaze
I wish I were a secret flash in his eye
or rare words forming on his still lips
I wish I were beside him like his shadow, with his every breath
Or staying up until dawn, longing for him to be close
Or surrendering to heart's hope, severing ties with parting—
shutting grief out, becoming moonlight from head to toe

Sarataan 1378 / Cancer 1999

شوق بی‌نیاز

من از دیار دوردست دوستی
به آشتی دهی شوق با نگاه آمدم
به التماس و لابه‌ها
زبان عاشقی شدم
سرودم این ترانه را
بیا یکی شویم باز هم
که جان‌پناه من تویی
نگو نگو نبوده‌ام
که جلوه‌گاه من تویی
به شب‌سرای خالی‌ام
بتاب! ماه من تویی

نگاه ناز می‌کند
امید طفره می‌رود
دو دست مهر نیز سست می‌شود
و من درین میانه شوق بی‌نیاز را
به دوش می‌کشم سبک
به دور می‌برم ازین کهن‌سرای دشمنی

سرطان ۱۳۸۰

Fantasy

I come from a distant land of friendship
to reconcile the eye with the heart
Begging, pleading
I use Love's tongue,
singing:
> *Let's become one again—*
>> *you were my refuge*
>
> *No, don't tell me I wasn't yours*
>> *You reflect every beauty*
>
> *In the empty night of my mind*
>> *you shine, my moon!*

But the eye fools
the heart tricks
Love's hands shake
So I hoist my small fantasy
onto my back
and spirit it away from this ancient place of bad blood

Sarataan 1380 / Cancer 2001

شکست

چه صادقانه، چه ساده
تو با یقین به شکفتن
درون حجرهٔ صبرت به انتظار نشستی
اگر بهار نیامد
تو با نسیم خیالت
لبی به خنده گشودی
و دل به آتیه بستی
ولی دریغ که هرگز
بهار در تو نجوشید
و بخت با تو نخندید
و تا به عشق رسیدی
بلای ظالم توفان
گل امید ترا چید
و ناشگفته شکستی

اسد ۱۳۸۰

Broken

How simple, how sincere
You were so sure of your blooming
        you sat in your foyer, expectant
Though spring didn't come
its breezes blew through your imagination
You laughed
        and set your heart on the future
But sadly
your spring never stirred
    and fortune didn't smile on you
        And when you found love
        the cruel disaster of that storm
        plucked your stem of hope
           and left you a bud, broken

Asad 1380 / Leo 2001

ناپیدا

مخمس برغزل «راز خون‌آلود» استاد سید ضیاءالحق سخا

افسوس کز دل‌های ما این عقده هرگز وا نشد
جشن سرور و آشتی در ملک ما برپا نشد
این چرخ کج‌رفتار یک‌ساعت به‌کام ما نشد
«بسیار شد کوشش ولی قفل در شب وانشد
یعنی کلید گم‌شده پیدا نشد، پیدا نشد»

از چشم‌های ابر، اشک قیرگون جاری شده
دست سپید ماهتاب از روشنی عاری شده
ظلمت‌سوار تیره‌دل سلطان این وادی شده
«گوئی که پشت کوه‌ها اسب سحر زخمی شده
کز هیچ سو هنگامه‌ای از هی هی فردا نشد»

تاریخ می‌داند که ما فرزند دریا بوده ایم
اینک چه معصومانه در مرداب‌ها آلوده ایم
ما پابرهنه ریگزار داغ را پیموده ایم
«فرسنگ‌ها فرسنگ‌ها پای خطر فرسوده ایم
اما به قدر یک قدم از خاک ما از ما نشد»

عمری‌ست در چشمان ما کس چشمهٔ عشقی ندید
صد خیمه زین خشکیدگی بر تن گریبان را درید
فریاد استستقا ما را خالق داور شنید
«صد آسمان غرید و هم صد ابر بارانی رسید
بارید و بارید و ولی برهوت ما دریا نشد»

خاکستری شد سرو، داغ نامرادی سوختش
با دست پرقدرت تبر بشکست و هی بفروختش
زین داغداری خاک، حسرت‌ها به دل اندوختش

Unnoticed

With lines from Sayed Ziaulhaq Sakhaa's "Bloody Secret"

This tragic knot is forever bound up in our hearts
There was no festival of joy and peace in our land—
that wheel of fortune didn't turn for even an hour of our delight
We tried many times, but the night's door didn't click open
        The lost key was never found, never found
The clouds cried pitch tears
The white hand of the moon was stripped of light
The dark-hearted rider in the night became the king of this valley
It is as if the horse of dawn lies wounded behind the mountain
        We call, but there is no answer
History knows we were children of the sea
Then we were poisoned by this swamp
We have crossed hot desert sands barefoot
For miles and miles its dangers have worn down our feet
        but we could not claim one inch of our land
It has been ages since anyone has spotted the well of love in our eyes
A hundred storm tents, miserable and useless, have torn their
    clothes in grief
Our just God heard our cries
A hundred skies thundered and a hundred storm clouds gathered
        It rained and rained—yet our wasteland did not become a sea
The cypresses greyed, charred by the hot stamp of ruin
Strong hands split them with the axe and sold them
Regrets piled in the heart of this hot, dry earth

«سبزه قباها دوختش، گل خنده‌ها آموختش
لاله چراغ افروختش، اما زمین زیبا نشد»
از حیله‌بازان فلک ترفندها آموختیم
ریگ گهرمانند را با حیله‌ها بفروختیم
در دفتر تاریخ بس افسانه‌ها اندوختیم
«از خون چراغ افروختیم بسیار دیده دوختیم
چشم تماشا سوختیم، اما کسی پیدا نشد»
فرسود عمر ما درین حسرت‌سرای بی‌نشان
هرگز نشد فارغ قلم از شرح اندوه وفغان
از دوردست دوستی وارد نشد یک کاروان
«پیدا نشد آن ساربان، آن ساربان راه‌دان
یا خود اگر آمد ولی جز در پی سودا نشد»
جام شرنگ عمر از بیچارگی نوشیده‌ایم
در دیگ هر ناپخته‌یی چون آب‌ها جوشیده‌ایم
در حل این پیچیده مشکل بارها کوشیده‌ایم
«این راز خون‌آلود را از آسمان پرسیده‌ایم
اما سکوت آسمان، روشن‌گر معنا نشد»

ثور ۱۳۸۰

The grass wove her dresses, the flower coached her to smile,
        the tulips shone their lights, but the earth was not beautiful
We learned tricks from the world's cheats
We sold glittering sand for the price of gems
We heaped stories on the book of history
We made lights with blood and fixed our gazes outward
        Our eyes began to burn, but no one came
Our lifetimes were run-down in this unnoticed land of regret
The pen never rested from telling our stories of sadness and wailing
No caravan arrived from the land of friendship
That camel rider, that camel rider who knew the path did not come
        If he did, he did his wicked business
We've drunk the poison of life with despair
We've been boiled in every idiot's pot
We've tried over and over to untangle this mess
We've asked the sky about this bloody secret
        but it is quiet—it sheds light on nothing

Sawr 1380 / Taurus 2001

سنگی

آمـدی بار دگر کز خویش بیزارم کنی
بشـکنی، برهم زنی و زغصه بیمارم کنی
آمدی کان آشـنایی را به یادم آوری
در بیـان خاطرات تلخ آزارم کنی
آمدی با دانه‌های تازه و دامی دگر
در حصـار تنگ زنجیرت گرفتارم کنی
من ترا سـنگی‌تر از قصاب ها دارم به‌یاد
با نوازش کی توانی باز افسـارم کنی
گوش هوش دل دگر با دوسـتی بیگانه است
کـی توانی بار دیگر یار و غمخوارم کنی
می‌گریـزم ازتو ای عاصی! رهایم کن، برو
بی‌گناهـم من، تو می‌خواهی گنهکارم کنی

دلو ۱۳۷۹

Like Flint

You came to make me hate myself
To break me, muddle me, make me sick with grief
You came to remind me of our friendship
and torture me with bitter memories
You came to lure me with new seeds and traps
to catch me in your tight chains
I remember—you are flintier than a butcher
You can't shackle me, can't fool me with flattery
My heart's sharp ears are far beyond amity
You won't make me your admiring pet again
I must run from you, you snake! Leave me, go
I am sinless, and you want to ruin me

Dalvæ 1379 / Aquarius 2001

نیزهٔ خورشید

دریچه را بگشا
آفتاب می‌تابد
به روی شب در بند
به شب بگوی که ما
بـه تاج دختر مهتاب جلوهٔ گُهریم
سـتارهٔ سحر از جنس گوشوارهٔ ماست

اگر فرود آیی
به داغ کورهٔ آتش‌فشـان سینهٔ ما
چو هیمه می‌سوزی
که آفتاب حقیقت به یک اشارهٔ ماست
اگر چه خسـته و بیچاره شب‌نشین شده ایم
به‌سان نیزهٔ خورشید
شکسـت آیینه شب هنوز چارهٔ ماست

دو چشم را واکن
ببین به اوج فلک
به آسـمان گهرخیز و کوکبان طلا
کـه لحظه لحظهٔ تار تو را فروغ دهند
چراغ خانهٔ تو
حدیث روشـنی قلب پر شرارهٔ ماست
قسـم به جلوهٔ رنگین کمان «هفت اورنگ»
که رنگ و روی زمان حسـن ماه‌پارهٔ ماست
به شب سلام مکن
صبح سبز نزدیک است

The Sun's Lance

Open the window—
                the sun burns
Shut out the night
Tell the night,
We are the gems nestled in the crown of the Moon's daughter
The morning stars adorn our ears

If you touch down
on the furnace of our molten chests
you will scorch like tinder
for the sun of truth rises at our call
Though we have become weary and wretched night-dwellers,
like the sun's lance, we can crack the mirror of night
and brace ourselves

Open both eyes
See the celestial heights,
the sky of gems, golden stars—
moment by moment, they will shine on you
Your lamplight
is the radiant tale of our sparking hearts
I swear on the rainbow of the "Seven Thrones"
that time's complexion is born of our moonlike beauty
Don't greet the night—
                the green morning is nearly here

شــب سیاه پر از وحشت است
تاریک است
بــه اوج عرش حقیقت، به مژدگانی مهر
به روی صبح بخند
به روی شب در بند

ثور ۱۳۷۸

Night is filled with dread,
                          is dark
From the height of Truth's peak, to the prophecy of love,
smile on dawn's face
shut out the night

Sawr 1378 / Taurus 1999

خواب‌گاه

افتاده کسی دیدم در حاشیهٔ جاده
خوابیده و فارغ بود از مال خداداده
ازکهنهٔ کرباسی پا تا کمرش پنهان
دیگر همه اندامش بر خاک تر افتاده
نه پای به کفش اندر نه جامه‌اش اندر بر
عریان بود و غافل بود از مردم ایستاده
هرکس ز سر تحقیر حرفی زده می‌خندید
سودازدهٔ اینش خواند، آن بی‌خبر از باده
آن جاهل و این غافل، آن مرده و این بیدل
هرکس که گذرکردی بر خفتهٔ دل ساده
بالای سرش بودم در بهت فرو رفته
کز روی زمین برشد ناگه سر بنهاده
چون جمع خلایق دید گفتا که چه بازارست
از بهر چه حیرانید؟ غولی مگر افتاده؟
گفتند کسانش ما، از حال تو حیرانیم
در حاشیه وارفتی ای هوش زکف داده
گر عقل به سر بودی این‌گونه نخوابیدی
لیلی‌صفتی شاید عقلت به فنا داده
گفتا چه می‌اندیشید بر مردک دیوانه
حیوان بیابان است این ژندهٔ افتاده
ازجامه چه می‌پرسید دیباست به تن ما را
اما نتواند دید چشمِ به گنه داده
آن کس که ز سر بگذشت در حسرت بالش نیست
باکی نبود ما را از خار و خس جاده
گر چشم به سر دارید، بالین مرا بینید

Bedroom

I saw a man in the gutter
sleeping with nothing
He was covered with an old rag
the rest of him bare on the wet ground
He had no shoes on his feet or clothing on his body,
exposed and unaware of the people gathered around him
They mocked the man, laughing
One person said he was crazy, another a drunk
One said he was an idiot, another ill, another dead, another lovesick
All who passed the man
stood above him, stupefied
Suddenly, he raised his head
Seeing the crowd, he asked, *What is this about?*
Why are you so shocked? Have you seen an ogre?
They told him, *We're baffled by your state*
Foolish man, you're sleeping on the side of the road
If you had any sense you wouldn't lie like this
Perhaps some Laila has wrecked your reason
He said, *Don't worry about this lunatic*
You think this shabby man is an animal of the wilderness
You ask about my clothes, but I am wearing silk
invisible to sinful eyes
The devout don't want cushions
I am unafraid of the road's thorns and shrubs
If you had eyes in your head, you would see my pillows

این خواب‌گهم بهتر از مخمل آماده
حیرت‌زده بنشستم برگل نظر افگندم
انگشت‌نما دیدم یک نقشهٔ سجاده

حمل ۱۳۷۸

This bed of mine is finer than woven velvet
I sat down, wide-eyed, looking at the flowers—
and I saw the pattern of a prayer rug

Hamal 1378 / Aries 1999

حسن خدایی

به هر کجا که رسیدم طلوع روی تو دیدم
ز شهرزاد خوش‌آوا، حکایت تو شنیدم

به هرچه شعر سرودم ترانه‌ساز تو بودی
خیال نقش تو بود آنچه روی صفحه کشیدم

اگر ز خلق گسستم چه غم که با تو نشستم
اطاعت تو گزیدم اگر ز جمع بریدم

به ظلمت شب سردم تو چل‌چراغ طلایی
طراوت گل صدرنگ شاخه‌های امیدم

شمیم دل‌کش جنگل، نسیم صبح بهاری
تو جلوهٔ شب شعرم، تو لطف بخت سپیدم

به بزم ماه‌لقایان، میان مجلس خوبان
به کبریایی حسن خدایی تو ندیدم

سرطان ۱۳۸۱

God-Given Beauty

Wherever I went I saw the dawn of your face
The sweet-singing Scheherazade told me your story

With each verse I wrote, you were the poet—
the marks on my pages the lines of your face

If I break away from the world, I sit calmly with you
If I'm cut off from the crowd, you are who I follow

In the gloom of my cold night, you are golden lights
On my hopeful branches' fresh peony blossoms, you are the dew,

the jungle's perfume, the spring morning's wind
You, my beautiful night of poetry—you, my silvery luck

At a banquet of lovely people, an elegant gathering,
I didn't find one rival to your noble God-given beauty

Sarataan 1381 / Cancer 2002

خفته در غبار

دردهای گنگ
دردهای دیرمانده در لفاف مبهم سکوت
در سرت قصیده‌های سوگبار خوانده اند
با نمایش کریه چهره‌های خویش
رنگ هستی ترا پرانده اند
آه
تو چقدر با تمام ساده‌گی غریب مانده‌ای
هیچ‌کس به زیرکی رشته‌های رنج
در رگان پیکر تو پی نمی‌برد
هیچ‌کس عنایتی به دقتی بزرگ
در نگاه مبهمت نمی‌کند
هیچ‌کس به هیچ‌کس
ترانهٔ شب لب ترا دوباره بازگو نمی‌کند
و خاک حتا
پیوند دیرسال ترا با خود انکار کرده است
چنان که حرف‌های کودکانه ات نگفته ماند
چنان که دفتر سرود های سرخوشانهٔ دل ترا کسی نخواند
هنوز خفته در غبار مانده‌ای
کسی سیاه‌پرده را
از استوای خانه‌ات نمی‌درد
کسی لبان بستهٔ ترا
به مهمانی شکفتن نگفته‌ها نمی‌برد
به آسمان سفر مکن
و در غم قشنگ هجر یک ستاره از مدار خویش
بی‌خودانه چشم تر مکن

Asleep in a Haze

Mute pains—

pains that have stayed in the dim sheets of silence for too long

They recite deadly elegies in your mind

By showing their ugly faces

they have made the color fade from your life

Ah

You have maintained your strange simplicity

No one notices the subtle threads of suffering

running through your veins

No one notes the great focus

in your odd stare

No one tells anyone

                of your nocturnal song

Even the soil

denies your ancient bond

Your childish thoughts remain unsaid

No one reads the book of your heart's joyful anthems

You are asleep in a haze

No one will tear the dark curtains

from the circle of your home

No one will invite your closed mouth

to the party where the silenced unfurl

Don't push off toward the sky

Don't cry at the beautiful pain

of a star leaving its course

که نیز ناز دخترانهٔ ترا
کسـی به یک نگاه جست‌وجوگر و عمیق آشنا نمی‌خرد
تو از مدار روزگار مانده‌ای

عقرب ۱۳۸۱

With your girlish coyness
no one will regard your gaze as probing and aware
so you are left outside life's orbit

Aqrab 1381 / Scorpio 2002

تبسم کاذب

حضور کند مرا کاهلی بهانه مکن
شعور تند مرا بی‌نمک ترانه مکن

پرم ز وسوسهٔ سرد سیر سورهٔ یأس
به سهم خویش، تو ام سوی شب روانه مکن

مرا که شادترین جلوه‌گاه امیدم
به عزم سفسطه تفسیر غمگنانه مکن

زبان زندهگی و انزجار، می‌دانم
تو زین بیانیه، تحلیل دشمنانه مکن

من از تبسم کاذب حکایتی دارم
قسم بخور به خدا، درد را فسانه مکن

درین دمی که نشستیم اختلاط کنیم
زمانه را تو به تن رخت شاعرانه مکن

حمل ۱۳۸۲

Fake Smile

Don't give me an excuse to laze
Don't turn my wit into a bland song

I am filled with the icy temptation of despair
Don't send me toward the night in your place

I am the happiest exhibition of hope
Don't read me as pitiful, you sophist

I know the language of life and hate
Don't take my speech as hostile

I know the story of a fake smile
Don't mythologize pain—swear to God you won't

In these moments when we sit to talk
don't dress your speech in esoteric poetry

Hamal 1383 / Aries 2004

بذر نوین

هرچه از سینهٔ این خاک برون می‌روید
بذر آفت زده‌یی‌ست
های آی دهقانان!
دیگر این کشت بداقبال سیه‌دوران را
آبیاری نکنید
آبیاری نکنید
بگذارید بسوزند و بمیرند همه
کشت آفت زده خوبست که ویران گردد
همه جا خاک و بیابان گردد
تاکه درآتیه دور و سپید
دست دهقان ازل
سربه‌سر بادیه را بذر نوین افشاند
بذری از باغ بهشت
دشت آفت‌زدگان باز گلستان گردد

قوس ۱۳۷۹

New Seeds

Everything that comes from this earth
                is from foul seeds
Farmers
of this cursed age of grim crops
        don't water them
        don't water them
                Let them all scorch and die
This blighted crop is best wasted,
        the land a dry desert
Then, in the pale faraway future
        the eternal farmer will use his hands
                scattering new seeds across this wasteland—
                seeds from heaven's fields
                Then these ruined plains will become gardens again

Qaws 1379 / Sagittarius 2000

کم‌رنگ‌ترین

آزار مکش! قفل دلم واشدنی نیست
تندیس تمنای تو پیداشدنی نیست

گنجینهٔ لطف تو بزرگ است، بزرگ است
در پیکرهٔ کوچک من جاشدنی نیست

راهی که فراروست دو خط متوازی‌ست
یعنی که حدیث من و تو ماشدنی نیست

توصیف مکن از خط و خالم، مفریبم
پروانهٔ پرسوخته زیباشدنی نیست

بی‌خود مده امید بلندم به بهاران
سروی که کمربُر شده، بالاشدنی نیست

شاید تو مسیحا شده ای، لیک مزن دم
دردی که دلم راست، مداواشدنی نیست

کم‌رنگ‌ترین واژهٔ دیوان حیاتم
درخط کج و ریز که خواناشدنی نیست

بگذار که ناخوانده و بیگانه بمیرد
این واژهٔ نفرین شده معناشدنی نیست

اسد ۱۳۸۱

The Most Faded Word

Don't bother! My heart's lock won't open
The figurine of your desire won't be found here

Your cache of kindness is large, large
My small frame won't hold it

There are two parallel paths ahead
Our two lives won't become a single story

Don't lie to me about my beauty
The burnt wings of a moth won't brighten

Don't give me hope for spring
A cypress tree cut at the waist won't regrow

You may have become the Messiah, but don't breathe on me
My heart carries a pain that won't be healed

I am the most faded word in the book of life
scrawled in a crooked script that won't be deciphered

Let it vanish, unread and unknown
This cursed word won't be understood

Asad 1381 / Leo 2002

وقتی

وقتی که چشم‌های تو غمگین اند
حس می‌کنم که در من
چیزی شکستنی‌ست
وقتی تو از نهایت قلبت گرفته‌ای
تا انجماد دلهره پرتاب می‌شوم
وانگاه اگر نگاه تو جریان کند به من
ناگه زخویش می‌روم و
آب می‌شوم

حوت ۱۳۸۱

The Moment

The moment your eyes show pain
I feel as if something inside me
                    will crack
When your heart aches
I am thrown into a paralyzing fear
And if your gaze flows over me
then all at once I will shatter
                    and vanish

Hoot 1381 / Pisces 2003

فرار

خســته شد دل‌های ما از دردها، بیچاره‌گی‌ها
گم شــدیم آخر میان خاک‌ها در تیره‌گی‌ها

می‌رویم این بار و ما را نیســت برگشت دوباره
ای خوشــا بگریختن از دست این بی‌هوده‌گی‌ها

مرغــی از باغ ارم بودیم اندر دام گیتی
بی‌گنــه ماندیم در دامان این آلوده‌گی‌ها

هر کســی آزرد با تیری پَر کوتاه ما را
بار دیگر نیســت ما را تاب این آزرده‌گی‌ها

دهــر زندان بود و ما در بند قفل آهنین
ای خوشــا بر ما که رستیم از حصار بنده‌گی‌ها

در تپش‌های مداوم نیســت دیگر اشتیاقی
خســته شد دل‌های ما از دردها، بیچاره‌گی‌ها

اسد ۱۳۷۹

Escape

Our hearts are tired of pain and misery
We ended up lost in the dirt, in darkness

We are leaving and won't return
We are lucky enough to escape this futility

We were a bird from Paradise, trapped in the world's net
We remained untainted despite this filthy trap

Someone shot our small wing with an arrow
We have no fight left for these tortures

We were locked in the prison of the world
We are lucky enough to escape this bondage

Our racing pulse is not fervor
Our hearts are tired of pain and misery

Asad 1379 / Leo 2000

تلاش باید کرد

غروب بود و خزان خیمه‌های زردش را
به صحن کوچه و باغ و چمن فراشته بود
درخت غم‌زده از شرِ تازیانهٔ باد
بهم شکسته و سرتا به پای می‌لرزید
و باغ عریان بود
در آن سکوت مداوم که درد می‌زایید
پرنده خسته و تنها نگاه سردش را
به آشیانهٔ ازهم‌گسسته دوخته بود
که دوش با خس و خاشاك کرد آبادش
و آرمید در آن با هزار عشق و امید
تگرگ تیرآسا
به‌جان خسته و خونین نیشتر می‌زد
پرنده نالان بود
شب ابرهای سیاه
ز هرکنار بر انوار ماه ره بستند
و باغ تیره و سرد
به سوگ دولت از دست‌رفته گریان بود
پرنده می‌ترسید
و از غریو پر از وهم جغد لرزان بود
چه تلخ بود ز غم کام مرغك مجروح
که باد خانهٔ زیبا و گرم و نرمش را
به‌یك اشاره چو بازیچه‌ای فنا می‌کرد
و مرغ کوچك را
به‌روی شاخهٔ بیدی ز جود می‌لرزاند
شبی گذشت و سحر شد
پرنده دیده گشود

We Must Try

It was dusk, autumn pitching yellow tents
on the courtyard, alley, garden, and grass
The cruel whipping wind ruined the tree,
now broken in on itself and shaking all over
The garden was naked
with a boundless, sorrowful silence
A single tired bird had fixed her cold eye
on the mangled nest she had woven
from twigs and straw the night before
and had nestled in with such pleasure
The rush of hail, like arrows,
had pierced her weary body bloody
The bird moaned
With nightfall, dark clouds
shut out every bit of the moon
The lightless frosty garden
wept with grief at the ruin
The bird was afraid,
trembling at the owl's awful cry
Her throat was hard with grief
With one wave of its finger
the wind had flung her snug home like a toy
The little hungry bird
shivered on a willow branch
Night passed into morning
The bird opened her eyes

و سوی شاخهٔ خالی نگاه برگرداند
که سرد و تیره و نمناک زیر باران بود
نه برگی و نه گلی
دو قطره اشک ز چشم پرنده بیرون زد
چه ناتوانم من!
پرنده پر زد و رفت
به‌سوی کشور بی‌انتهای رنج و محن
به اوج تنهایی
ز باغ خالی و بی‌هم‌نفس گریزان بود
بهار بود و درختان به صد کرشمه و ناز
سرود می‌خواندند
گل سپید عرق کرده بود و باد سحر
به صحن باغ و چمن مشک تازه می‌پاشید
پرستوان همه میهمان بوستان بودند
فضا معطر و پروانه پای‌کوبان بود
پرنده عزم سفر کرد و رخت بست و برفت
پرنده پای به شهر نوین نهاد و نشست
به زیر گنبد نیلی و آفتابی و صاف
به هر طرف چمنی دید سبز و روح‌نواز
نگاه کرد به مرغان شاد خوش‌بختی
که در میان درختان ترانه‌خوان بودند
پرنده ناگه ازین تازگی به وجد آمد
به خنده با خود گفت:
چو عمر در گذر است
و اعتنا نکند بر سیاه‌روزی من
چرا به خویش نپردازم و غمین باشم
تلاش خواهم کرد
دوباره لانه‌یی از عشق و نور خواهم ساخت

and stared at the bare branch

cold, dark, and wet, hanging from rain

with no leaf or flower

Two tears fell from her eyes

How powerless I am!

The bird shot up

to the vast land of pain and woe

to the peak of loneliness

trying to flee the empty garden

Then, it was spring—trees made one hundred coy gestures

humming their songs

Flower's pearly glow and dayspring's breeze

sprinkled perfume on the garden's face

The swallows were the garden's guests

The air was sweet, the butterflies whirling

Deciding to go, the bird gathered herself, and left

She set off to a new place and touched down

under the blue dome, clear and shining

Everything around her was green and thrilling

She peered at the lively birds of fortune

singing in the trees

She rejoiced in the newness

She laughed to herself,

Life goes on

with no concern for my sadness

Why not care for myself and be content

I will try

I will build a home of love and light

به اوج ناژوها
به جای امن که دست عقاب‌ها نرسد
به گوشهٔ مستور
که باد هم نتواند به خاکش اندازد
به سوی کشور امید رفت ولانه گزید
و آرمید از آن چون شهی به قصر سپید
و باز زمزمه کرد
زمانه در گذراست
واعتنا نکند بر سیاه‌روزی من
تلاش باید کرد

جدی ۱۳۷۸

in the height of the pines
in a safe place eagles cannot reach
in a shielded corner
Even the wind won't throw it down
She flew to the land of hope and wove a nest
settling like a king in a white palace
She sang,
Life goes on
with no concern for my sadness
yet we must try

Jaddi 1378 / Capricorn 1999

برگ‌های صبر

میهن طلوع صبح سعادت مبارکت
پایان روزگار مذلت مبارکت
آخر دعای نیمه‌شبان مستجاب شد
انوار آفتاب اجابت مبارکت
شاخ بزرگ صبر تو آخر شکوفه کرد
جریان مشک‌سای طراوت مبارکت
بر درد بی‌دوای تو درمان رسیده است
سالم شدی، وجود سلامت مبارکت
دوران تلخ‌کامی‌ات اینک به‌سر رسید
شهدت به کام گشت حلاوت مبارکت
ایمان راستین تو ره بر نفاق بست
دستان با ارادهٔ وحدت مبارکت
پائیز زرد رفت و شب سرد نیز رفت
سبزینه فصل شور و حرارت مبارکت

قوس ۱۳۸۰

The Leaves of Patience

Motherland, praise your dawn of glory
Praise the end of this shameful era
Finally, your prayer in the dead of night was answered
Praise the sun's rays of kindness
Finally, your great branch of patience blooms
Praise the sweet breeze
You shook off boundless pain
Praise your whole, cured form
The time of misery is over
Praise your honey-sweetened mouth
Your faith shut out spite
Praise those assured hands of peace
The biting autumn ceased, so did the icy night
Praise this green season of feeling and warmth

Qaws 1380 / Sagittarius 2001

هنگامه

باز تنها منم و جلوهٔ زیبایی شب
باز عاشق شده ام عاشق تنهایی شب
باز مردم همه خوابیده و من مست خیال
جام‌ها برده ام از ساقی رؤیایی شب

وه چه زیباست که با دیدهٔ دل می‌بینم
باز مهتاب مرا «دختر من» می‌خواند
دعوتم می‌کند از لطف به جان‌خانهٔ خویش
و به صد ناز و ادا سوی وطن می‌خواند

باز پیرامن دل وسوسه‌ها حلقه زدند
که ازین غمکده بیرون ببرم مایهٔ جان
شاد پرواز کنم سوی افق‌های سپید
بدر آرم ز قفس گنج گران‌مایهٔ جان

گر ازین تیره‌سرا رخت ببندم چه عجب
خانه‌ام گوشه‌یی از ماه خدا خواهد شد
روح من تا دل انوار خدا خواهد رفت
دل من مأمن آیات بقا خواهد شد

مرغ بی‌بال و پرم شوق پریدن دارم
دیده بر دست توانای که باید دوزم
گر کسی نشکند این حلقهٔ پولادین را
لاجرم در عطش وسوسه‌ها می‌سوزم

Turmoil

Once more I'm alone in the beauty of night
Once more I'm in love, in love with its solitude
Once more everyone is asleep and I'm drunk with thoughts
The night gives me many glasses to drink

The beauty of seeing with the heart's eye
Once more the moon calls me *daughter*
She invites me sweetly to her
A hundred times she coaxes me to come home

Once more temptations circle my heart
to pluck my soul from this sad place
I fly freely, facing white horizons
I lift my precious life from this cage

If I leave this darkness, know my home
will be in the crook of God's moon
My soul will climb to the center of God's light
My heart will be a refuge for signs of life

I am a wingless bird that hopes to fly
Which strong hand should I look to for help
If no one breaks this iron chain
I will burn with temptation's thirst

تو مرا تا به سرانجام توانی بردن
آه، ای شعر فسون‌کار مددکاری کن
بی‌وجود تو به دل این‌همه هنگامه بوَد
تو مرا وسوسه کردی، تو مرا یاری کن

جدی ۱۳۷۹

You take me to the brink,

charming poem—help me

Without you, my heart is in turmoil

You lured me in, now save me

Jaddi 1379 / Capricorn 2000

محزون‌ترین سروده

من درفضای باور خود دود می‌شوم
آرام پیچ‌خورده و نابود می‌شوم
تا دست‌های دلهره می‌پرورد مرا
در قعر خواب‌ها تپش‌آلود می‌شوم
واندم به عزم حفرهٔ دیرآشنای خاک
پا در رکاب لحظهٔ موعود می‌شوم
گاهی زعشق خشک و سراب‌آفرین ابر
سوزان‌ترین کویر نمک‌سود می‌شوم
اما خیال چشمه چو تر می‌کند مرا
در بستر عطش زدهگی رود می‌شوم
گر سر نخی رسد به من از رشتهٔ امید
بر تارهای نازک دل پود می‌شوم
این بی‌وداع رفته خیال‌آور من است
باز این منم که خاطره‌اندوه می‌شوم
شب نیز کم کمک ره خود می‌رود و من
محزون‌ترین سرودهٔ بدرود می‌شوم

حوت ۱۳۸۱

The Most Solemn Verse

I become smoke in my faith's atmosphere
Slowly I twist and turn, then become nothing
While anxious hands care for me,
I become a pounding in the void of sleep
Then, aiming for that familiar ditch of earth,
I become the rider loping toward the fated moment of death
When love is dry, a mirage of clouds,
I become the hottest salt desert
And yet if the memory of spring touches me
I become a river in the bed of thirst
If one strand of hope finds me
I become woven on my heart's thin threads
But my muse left with no goodbyes
and, again, I become the memory of grief
The night also leaves, little by little,
and I become the most solemn verse of farewell

Hoot 1381 / Pisces 2003

ای‌کاش

الا ای دختران انزوای قرن
الا ای راهبان ساکت بیگانه با مردم
الا ای مرده در آیین لب‌ها تان تبسم
بی‌صدا در کنج مهجوری خزیده
با تبار خاطرات خفته در انبوه حسرت‌ها
اگر در لابلای یادها لبخند را دیدید
بگوییدش:
تمنای شکفتن نیست لب‌ها را
ولی ای‌کاش در جریان اشک‌آرای نجواهای مان
گاهی
سخن را جلوهٔ کم‌رنگ می‌بخشید

قوس ۱۳۸۰

If

Oh daughters of a century's seclusion—
mute nuns, strangers
with smiles dead to the religion of your lips—
you silently crawled to a dark nook
        with a tribe of memories dozing under a heap of regrets
If you find a smile pressed among your thoughts
tell it:
> We don't hope for our lips to bloom
> But in the stream of our teary whispers
>   one day, Smile,
>   give our words some color

Qaws 1380 / Sagittarius 2001

Diana Arterian:
On Translating Nadia Anjuman

> You take me to the brink,
> charming poem—help me
> ...You lured me in, now save me
> —Nadia Anjuman

I learned about Nadia Anjuman like most Westerners did: through international news sources relaying the details of her death. It troubles me that, for me and so many, her tragedy preceded her words, that it was her death that grabbed me and provoked me to learn about her and find the snippets of rough English translations online. I then began to translate a few of Anjuman's poems with the aid of Persian-speaking friends. These friends would often weep or feel gripped with terror while reading the originals. The power of her poems was clear; Anjuman's tragic death was not the only or primary cause of the international response to her murder. She was beloved in her community—a kind, generous force there—and her poetry was remarkable and well-known. It was thus no surprise that the details of Anjuman's murder reached beyond Afghanistan's borders.

At the time I began this work, I hadn't questioned my right to translate these poems. I was young and unaware of some of the anti-colonial thinking about translation that would later make clear to me the problematic implications of my project. After all, I was an Anglo-Westerner with no knowledge of Persian translating the work of a contemporary Afghan poet who had died because of domestic violence.

While holding no explicit ties to the region by heritage, as an American I am undeniably connected to Afghanistan. Indeed, I am connected to any region the United States has invaded and where it has wreaked havoc in the name of "liberty" and "democracy."

Afghanistan, in particular, was subject to what Shahnaz Khan dubs "colonial feminism"—a practice in which governmental power(s) invoke the plights of women for militaristic propaganda, though ultimately these same women make up the majority of casualties, or what that same military would call "collateral damage."* As one Afghan woman said, "The Americans did not bring us any rights. They just came, fought, killed, and left." Anjuman's murder, for many, was particularly heinous. Her husband beat her to death after the U.S. involvement in Afghanistan—which supposedly aimed to help "liberate" Afghan women—had been dubbed a "success" by the U.S. itself.

A woman dying at the hands of her spouse or intimate partner is an epidemic hardly contained to "developing" or Islamic countries. In the summer of 2016, at the time when I first drafted this note, the United States—the self-defined premier nation in the Western "developed world"—was wrapping up one of the more brutal and horrific weeks of femicide by current or former romantic partners, with eight deaths (that made it to major news outlets) in seven days. The victims' ages ranged from fifteen to seventy-nine. One was over eight months pregnant. All involved close-encounter deaths—these women were beaten, strangled, mutilated, shot, set on fire, or stabbed by men with whom they were, at one time or another, romantically entangled. The U.S. Department of Justice recently put out a document entitled "Female Victims of Violence," based on research from 2007. According to the data at that time, 45% of all female murder victims in the United States were killed by an intimate partner. Non-deadly physical and verbal abuse is, of course, far more prevalent. This is all to say, the manner of Anjuman's death is hardly a "third world problem"—and to suggest that similar deaths illustrate a need for U.S. invasion is patronizing and hypocritical.

---

* Shahnaz Khan. 2008. "Afghan Women: The Limits of Colonial Rescue." In *Feminism and War: Confronting U.S. Imperialism*: 161-178. London: Zed Books.

How my government comported itself in Afghanistan was defined by violence. The American military hounded, tortured, and imprisoned many Afghans (including in Guantanamo Bay). They hunted people down based on any information that came their way. As one man tortured by Americans on a phony tip put it, "There was no one left standing in the end. It was as if the whole system just devoured everyone." In 1979, when the Soviet Union invaded Afghanistan, it had been by and large a peaceful country. After Soviet occupation and the American military's embroilment, as Anand Gopal writes in his excellent *No Good Men Among the Living: America, the Taliban, and the War Through Afghan Eyes*, Afghanistan was left "one of the most war-ravaged nations on Earth." Once the American military ousted the Taliban, it pursued former Talibs to brutal extremity despite the fact that the majority had returned their arms and were actively pro-Hamid Karzai (the U.S.-backed president). As one Afghan man put it, "no human being would do what those animals did."

All of this swirls in the background of this book, and I tried to keep it present in my mind throughout the years it took to complete it. Once I had decided to seriously pursue translating Anjuman, I realized that I needed someone to work closely with who could provide literal English translations of the poems. For generations, this practice has been relatively common for English-language writers attempting to translate works from non-Western languages without fluency or even rudimentary knowledge. In such cases, translators have applied a veneer of their own culture over the source text, or not given any credit to those who provided literals. Some have wildly mistranslated work, often because they have ignored an author's literary lineage. Because of the fraught history of this practice, I wanted to create as ethical a relationship as possible with my co-translator: to pay for their work, to allow as much collaboration as the co-translator desired, and to ensure that both of our names were associated with subsequent publications. I knew that I needed more from the co-translator than just the literal meaning. I needed to be informed of Persian sayings and Islamic concepts in the background of Anjuman's texts that might elude me despite my own research.

Marina Omar was, in so many ways, an ideal partner in the project. She translated for Afghan refugees some years ago before pursuing her education in the States, where she earned her PhD and now lives and works. She was born in Afghanistan at roughly the same time as Anjuman, growing up under Taliban rule. Like Anjuman, she eventually attended a university there. Her experience and knowledge were hugely important to the translation. Beyond all this, I felt it was important to work with another woman. Much of Anjuman's writing points to an environment that at times severely curbed women's agency, even endangering them physically. Anjuman's tragedy was so bound up in her gender, and it felt vital that we were a translation team of two women—and that one of us had first-hand experience of being a woman in Afghanistan.

Our first task was to translate a handful of pieces to use in grant applications. After obtaining funding, we began translating together in earnest. We would send each poem back and forth until we agreed we had understood Anjuman's poetic intentions. Through text documents and email, Marina sent me literal translations, which I printed and worked on. I often got caught on a snag—a word in a line with many potential meanings, or a whole line with complex grammar that left me confused. I sent my version back, the snags in bold, a list of questions. Just as often, I came across a phrase I didn't understand, which Marina then explained (as in the line in "Unnoticed" that references a cultural practice of tearing one's collar as a sign of protest).

Despite my inability to read the original Persian, this translation process created a sense of intimacy with Anjuman's poems. As poet and translator Don Mee Choi, alluding to the work of Deleuze and Guattari, writes, "Translation is a map, a mode that can trigger endless crossings from one party to another, 'neither of whom has seen.'" Anjuman's original lines whirled in a void, with Marina pulling out threads and handing them to me, helping me weave them together, close up the remaining holes. A family friend from Iran (Fariba Sirjani) went through an advanced draft of the manuscript to ensure the final co-translations were accurate, ultimately imparting even more of Anjuman's nuance.

Reflecting on the decade-plus I devoted to working with Marina, researching, and editing this collection, I think of Joyelle McSweeney and Johannes Göransson's "Manifesto of the Disabled Text," where they write: "Translation is not only the text rendered into a new language; it is the entire operation." For me, this extended process is best described through similes of embodied experience. In his frequently quoted "Task of the Translator," Walter Benjamin proposes that,

> [u]nlike a work of literature, translation does not find itself in the center of the language forest but on the outside facing the wooded ridge; it calls into it without entering, aiming at that single spot where the echo is able to give, in its own language, the reverberation of the [original] work. (Tr. Harry Zohn)

Or, per Anne Carson, translation is "a room, not exactly an unknown room, where one gropes for the light switch."

This endless calling into the woods, fumbling for something just out of reach, perhaps surprisingly, is one of the most vital modes of creative engagement I have experienced. Discomforts and inevitable failures are a defining feature of the enterprise of translation, and one you ultimately must accept, continually, at every juncture. This mode of creativity feels antithetical to the common approaches that are defined by drive yoked to self-importance (how else can someone approach a blank canvas or page without simply crumpling under the pressure?). The specificity of translation is best described by Eliot Weinberger: "In its way a spiritual exercise, translation is dependent on the dissolution of the translator's ego: an absolute humility toward the text."

Had I had more translation knowledge when Marina and I began, I would have requested a "trot"—the literal translations with the different connotative meanings of certain words denoted by slashes (e.g. "race/hurry/sprint"). Marina was not providing me with anything nearly as tight, and I was then unaware of the trot as a keystone to literary translation. So we felt through each of the poems slowly, with me worrying over words and idiomatic phrases. I realize that describing our practice puts into relief how messy it was. Yet this was my first attempt at translation of this sort—I was learning as I went along—and poetry is rarely simple. Ultimately, I'm grateful for our process, as it kept us at a meditative pace. I had to work intimately with every poem, contemplating each word, sending questions to Marina if the meaning of her literal translation was opaque to me. Throughout this co-translation process, I kept Anjuman at the forefront of my mind. I hoped, above all, that we were honoring her remarkable dedication to her verse. Even when some lines were weaker in comparison to others, my responsibility in maintaining the shortcomings felt equally important. She cannot be flawless. This collection demonstrates her power (I think of the mature insights of "Accept the Truth," which Anjuman wrote when only seventeen years of age; the elegance of "The Night of Poetry"), alongside her poetic experiments that may not have operated with as much intensity as she had hoped. She died so young; this editorial decision feels important to show the work of someone who was still mapping her aesthetic landscape.

While I wanted first and foremost to represent Anjuman's intentions, a translating poet cannot work in a vacuum—to some degree the translator's own voice mingles with that of the original poet. Translation is often a collaboration between author and translator (versus, say, a transliterator). Benjamin writes in "On Language as Such and on the Language of Man," "Translation is removal from one language into another through a continuum of transformations" (tr. Edmund Jephcott). This calls to mind a translator who described to me their belief that infinite translations of a work exist—through the act of translation, in the mind of the translator. In this work, I wanted to shake off any impulse to needlessly infuse lyricism into the poems, particularly lyricism defined by Romantic conventions of poetry. English translators have been applying a layer of Western poetic customs on non-Western work and society for centuries. I have no interest in participating in such oppressive aesthetic practices. After many iterations of this manuscript, my hope is that it reads as simultaneously modern and entrenched in a particular poetic tradition—just as Anjuman was herself.

At times I maintain the original Persian words in Roman characters because their specificity felt important, often fully explicated in notes at the end of the collection. I recognize that this gesture may read as problematic. In some translations, this serves to continually denote that the poet from a foreign land is just that, potentially exoticizing them by translating particular idioms or terms literally, or including non-English words. Oftentimes this leads to wooden translations that clearly have little interest in conveying the spirit of the original work, but rather the novelty of the culture of the original author to a person not from that place. This is far from my intention. My goal here is to provide a book for someone akin to myself: a Western English reader who is unable to read Persian. I hope the reader, like myself, is open and interested in Afghanistan's rich and ancient culture. It is one that has been ubiquitous in U.S. media since our invasion and nevertheless inscrutable. Anjuman's work is thus a means of access to a particular voice that has been consistently forced silent by regime after regime, and then pigeonholed by Western media outlets and governments as nothing more than the voice of the oppressed in need of saving. She was a devout Muslim woman, and radical in her artistic practice. Poetry by such a person, written during the period in which Anjuman lived and worked, is nothing short of a gift, and—though this is not a responsibility one such as Anjuman should bear—a potential site of education for those in the West who remain woefully ignorant about people from her part of the world. (Anglophone access to such writing will likely only become more difficult, considering recent events.) Beyond this, however, Anjuman's writing illustrates the ancient history of Afghan and Persian literature—how Afghanistan and its citizens are not defined by the Soviet Union's and United States' violence within its borders.

Just a few years ago, after twenty years of war, the United States military left Afghanistan. The last American soldier left on August 30, 2021. This war came at the cost of the likely significantly underreported 47,000 Afghan civilians' lives, as well as the American and Taliban soldiers killed. After all this time and loss, whatever "gains" one might argue the American military accomplished were overwhelmed in a mere nine days. There are innumerable reasons for this: President Trump had undermined American officials in negotiation with the Taliban by announcing American troop removal prematurely; President Ghani did not have any leverage during negotiations with the Taliban; the Taliban essentially decided to do whatever they wanted. Ultimately, the U.S. disastrously injected itself into a country seized by internal conflict. It was wild to see American conservatives and liberals come together to try to extract Afghan women, girls, and other persons of interest from the country, though perhaps with different understandings of what fostered such a dire situation.

The implications of our military's actions will likely be something we try to untangle for decades. Because of the extent of our involvement and the amount of time we spent in the country, the Afghan economy is inextricably connected to U.S. military presence. There has been no financial support for Afghans in the wake of U.S. military removal, because most countries will not supply aid to a "terrorist-run nation." Civilians took to selling whatever goods they had to make ends meet. Mahmad Akbar, a seller of such used materials, told the *Washington Post*,

> Only three times in my life have I seen the situation this bad. The first time was about 30 years ago, when the Russians left and the mujahideen came and fighting broke out. The second was about 20 years ago, when the Taliban took over and people ran away. This is the third.

Several articles catalog the ways in which Afghans in rural areas felt remarkable relief at American absence. In the first six months of 2021, close to 5,200 rural civilians died during the conflict between the U.S. military and the Taliban. Drone strikes habitually killed innocent people, often with little regard from my government unless the deaths received public outcry. You have likely read about these events: drones that hit hospitals, weddings, schools. "Thank God the Americans went away," one man in rural Kulangār said. Mohammed Omar, an imam in a village, went so far as to say, "The major change is there is peace and security now, and the killings of the people have stopped. You can move freely now anywhere. Death has disappeared."

In the fall of 2021, when my friends shook their heads at the U.S. being involved at all in Afghanistan, I found myself agreeing with them—but also, of course, thinking about Anjuman. How she would never have gone to college, perhaps never been published or won awards for her poems, without the U.S. pushing the Taliban out of the cities. And she is just one person, one life among over 40 million. I still don't have easy or uncomplicated feelings about any of this, and likely never will. One woman in a rural village told a journalist, regarding the U.S. military invasion, "They are giving rights to Kabul women, and they are killing women here." The division of experience between urban and rural Afghans over the last twenty years is immense, with some villagers losing dozens of family members during my government's active violence there.

Overall, I feel sick over U.S. aggression in Afghanistan, which preceded both Anjuman's lifetime and mine. The U.S., as we so often do, played a huge role in creating the past and current tumult in another country. I am sick over our meddling in the Soviet conflict there in the seventies, exploiting Afghanistan as a theater of Cold War engagement. (We funded and armed the mujahideen to beat back the Soviets in the 1970s. Once the Soviets were gone, the U.S. halted support. A subsequent civil war erupted due to the warring factions within the mujahideen—some of whom ultimately became the Taliban, which became a dominant governing power in the country.) I'm sick at the staggeringly deadly costs for whatever supports the last two decades of U.S. involvement did actually provide. And sick over how quickly those supports buckled, illustrating the lack of substantive interest or capacity to provide something long lasting to a nation we have harmed so thoroughly over two generations. A tiny portion of the $145 billion the U.S. spent in Afghanistan went to infrastructure or governance. As Gopal writes, "The rest was mostly military expenditure, a significant chunk of which ended up in the coffers of regional strongmen."

In an interview with an American journalist held a few months before U.S. troops withdrew, Mahbouba Seraj, a septuagenarian activist who runs a women's shelter in Kabul, said,

> I have a belief in the energy and the idea of the newness and the commitment of the young people of this country ... So many women and so many young people, so full of energy. They're not going to give this up.

Women protested in Badakhshan province. More protesters demonstrated in Anjuman's home city of Herat. All involved beatings and, for some, even death. One protestor held a poster that read in English: "Why the world is watching us silently and cruelly?"

After U.S. withdrawal, Afghan resistance movements fought hard to keep the Taliban from regaining a complete grip on the country. The National Resistance Front held the Panjshir province near Kabul far longer than any might have expected. These Afghans resisted and still resist, despite the multitudinous ways in which they have been disastrously harmed and underserved by my country.

After the Taliban takeover in 2021, women posted videos online in which they sang poems as resistance while dressed in burqas, making them unidentifiable. Some of them sang Anjuman's poems. Girls still held out hope that they could return to school beyond sixth grade. They participated in clandestine lessons and classes, much like Anjuman had at the Golden Needle School, but online. The Taliban have only restricted them further. In the fall of 2024, the Taliban announced their most draconian morality code, or "vice and virtue law," which banned women from singing, speaking, or reading in public, among other terrifying restrictions. In response, Afghan women worldwide posted videos of themselves singing online. But those who remain in Afghanistan, the young girls especially, are devastated by the clear foreclosure of their futures. The online education groups have faltered, afraid of retribution. An E.U. top court recently ruled Afghan women applying for asylum need only prove their gender and nationality to receive it. One Afghan woman, a 48-year-old women's rights activist, sees the experiences of her youth repeated today. "The entire country has turned into a graveyard for women's dreams," she said.

As we translated and sent poems to journals, applied for grants, and spoke to people about Anjuman, I grew increasingly concerned that most were attracted to her painful narrative rather than her incredible poetry. While the events surrounding Anjuman's struggle and death are undeniably important, we must avoid the common tropes of the tragic young genius, the dead woman writer, the oppressed foreign woman. Her suffering should not eclipse the brilliance of her verse. She was a woman of faith. She was a lover of literature. Her work crackles. I hope that Anjuman's poetry will be the first point of contact, rather than her death; that more people will learn of her writing and translate her poems.

It's equally important to keep in mind that these poems don't always tell Anjuman's personal story. Afghan and Persian poetry, the tradition in which Anjuman worked, often employs a roving "I," or persona. The desire to attach each poem in the collection to Anjuman's life is based largely on Western poetic reading practices in which the speaker and the writer are deemed to be one and the same. Anjuman is not so easily pinned down. This is not to say that she is not engaging deeply with personal experiences in these pieces, but rather that our desire to access her narrative from her poetry will likely be fruitless. The intimacies of her existence are reserved for those who were close to her in life.

The poems that seem most personal to me are those that illustrate her deep love of writing poetry, as well as her desire to conjure up hope despite her difficult situation, whether as a teenager under Taliban rule or in her marriage. Those pieces that address injustice head-on and seem to concern her own oppression rather than that of an invented figure come at the reader through the gut, sure and terrifying. I think especially of the thrillingly triumphant poem, "A Story." After attacks and silence and trials, the speaker states, "This is I! She who speaks." Indeed—through her verse and actions, Anjuman's words endure.

Anjuman's brother, S., was arguably her biggest advocate, paying to publish his sister's poetry collections in Afghanistan. He has also been the arbiter of her estate, so we have been in contact for some years. Recently, a Portuguese publisher reached out to me to ask about publishing Anjuman's work in a Persian/Portuguese collection. I put the publisher and S. in touch, and he provided permission. At this point, S. and I were emailing often, as I was increasingly worried about his safety. Not only had he published

Anjuman's work, which women were actively using as a means of resistance online, he also worked for nonprofits for women, was a professor, and had several other characteristics that very likely made him a person of interest for the Taliban. He was struggling to gain any traction with the German nonprofit he had worked for, and the U.S. gave me no hope for getting him to this country despite the precarity of his safety. I mentioned to the publisher that S. and his family were in need of refuge, and he advocated for them in Portugal. Incredibly, the publisher was successful. S., his wife, and their two young children were able to safely relocate as refugees. Of course, resettling as a refugee in a country where one doesn't know the language, culture, or have connections to locals brings with it many complications. S. had to leave behind his home, his mother, his loved ones and friends. What is touching to me, however, is how Anjuman's poetry helped shepherd her brother's family to physical safety. The power of Anjuman's poems—her power—is undeniable, vital, and active despite her death almost twenty years ago.

Marina Omar:
On Translating Nadia Anjuman

When Diana Arterian approached me to co-translate the poems from Nadia Anjuman's two collections, *Flower of Smoke* (گل دودی, *Gul-e-Dodi*) and *A Basket of Doubt* (یک سبد دلهره, *Yek Sàbad Délhoreh*), I felt a fluttering sensation in my chest. Anjuman's poems expressed a pain that I too had experienced but been neither brave nor talented enough to express. I too had suffered the cruelty of the ban by the Taliban on female education and the intolerance of Afghan society for any expression of women's plight. Translating Anjuman's poems required immense courage that I wasn't sure I had. Nonetheless I was determined to master that courage and to make Anjuman's voice heard beyond the boundaries of the Farsi-speaking world. Making her work available to more people would be a way to redeem myself for being too timid to express the agony I had felt during those dark years. I lived in Kabul in 1996 when the Taliban took over the capital and prohibited women from working and going to school.

Translating poetry is a difficult task. The translator is faced with the challenge of conveying the nuances and devices that make poetic language unique: its symbols, metaphors, and rhythm. My command of both Farsi and English allowed me to provide a literal translation of Anjuman's poems. As luck would have it, my co-translator, Diana Arterian, is a talented poet herself, and she was able to give the literal translations their poetic form. Putting our skills together, Diana and I tried to tackle the task of conveying Anjuman's message such that nothing, or at least not a lot, was lost in translation.

My graduate-school schedule dictated that I do my translating at night, after my classes and teaching responsibilities. The darkness of the night provided a relentless backdrop that suited the tone in Anjuman's poems. As I translated on, however, that darkness gave way to a flickering light that became only stronger as I continued reading. Anjuman writes: "I am closing the door on grief, becoming moonlight from head to toe," and, indeed, she became the moonlight, illuminating the darkest nights of women in the darkest corners of Afghanistan.

Moonlight cannot be contained in a single geographical place. This book will let Anjuman's light shine on and brighten many more hearts. Readers will accompany Anjuman on her journey as they read her poems and see the unceasing flame that she lit up in her twenty-five years of life, a brilliant life that was violently cut short. I will end this note with one of my favorite verses from Anjuman:

> Morning, don't tear at the silk of my illusion
> I swear to the night—it kindles my thoughts

November 1, 2024, Virginia, USA

Chronology

1978 Soviet occupation of Afghanistan begins

1979 Soviet War in Afghanistan begins

1980 Nadia N., aka Nadia Anjuman, is born in Herat (Dec. 27)

1985 Anjuman begins attending elementary school

1986 Anjuman writes her first poem

1989 Soviet occupation ends

1992 Herat's governor, Ismail Khan, declares himself ruler of western Afghanistan

1995 The Taliban begin to gain power and a following in Afghanistan
Extensive drought throughout Afghanistan begins
The Taliban take over Herat and ban women and girls from schools

1996 Anjuman begins attending Golden Needle School to continue her education in literature and poetry in secret
The Taliban take over Kabul

2001 The United States' "Operation Enduring Freedom" begins (October)
The Taliban lose control of the country (November)
Drought ends with major snowfall

2002 Anjuman begins attending the University of Herat

2004 Anjuman marries

2005 Gul-e-Dodi (Flower of Smoke) is published in Afghanistan under the pen name Nadia Anjuman. Derived from the ancient Pahlavi language, انجمن (Anjuman) means community, association, or group.
Anjuman gives birth to a son
Yek Sàbad Délhoreh (A Basket of Doubt) is set for publication in Afghanistan and Iran
Anjuman dies at the age of 24 (Nov. 4, Eid al-Fitr)

2006 Yek Sàbad Délhoreh (A Basket of Doubt) is published

2020 U.S.–Taliban deal signed, promising U.S. military removal

2021 The Taliban begin a major offensive in Afghanistan (May 1)
The vast majority of U.S. military personnel leave Afghanistan (July)
The Taliban succeed in taking over Kabul; President Ashraf Ghani flees Afghanistan (Aug. 15)

The United States military fully evacuates from Afghanistan (Aug. 30)
The Taliban ban co-education, close girls' schools beyond sixth grade, and ban women from secondary education (September)

2024 A Taliban manifesto decrees women cannot speak, sing, or read in public

2025 The Taliban bans all literature written by women from university curricula

Notes to the Poems

Persian and Sufi literature, two of the most ancient literatures in the world, have reached far outside the modern boundaries of Iran for over two millennia. (Rumi, one of the most famous Persian poets, was likely born in what is now Afghanistan.) The imagery in Anjuman's poems, explained below, often draws from this rich lineage. Quotations from poems are translations by Annemarie Schimmel in *A Two-Colored Brocade: The Imagery of Persian Poetry*.

At the bottom of each of her poems, Anjuman notes the date based on the Afghan Persian calendar, which is derived from the signs of the Zodiac. We have given these dates as well as their Julian calendar equivalents.

In Vain

Traditionally in the ghazal form the first two lines and final line of each subsequent couplet bear the same ending (usually a word or phrase). Because of the differing syntaxes of Persian and English, the repetition in this English translation ("I") falls at the beginning or near-beginning of these lines.

howl— The word translated here as "howl" is pronounced *faghan*. Anjuman is pointing to the similarity between *Afghan* and *faghan* here.

Peace

storm— While normally life-giving, storms also bring the potential danger of flood.

Red Majesty

In this translation, the ghazal's repetition ("we realized") falls at the beginning of the line.

pomegranate— This poem is about New Year's celebrations (in spring in Afghanistan), when people visit each other. As the figures sit close together, they realize they are like pomegranate seeds and recognize the refined dignity of that intimacy. Pomegranates have many potential associations, including the open heart disclosing its secrets.

clear heart— A clear heart, one that can reflect beauty and/or truth, with the idea of interiority as reflection, is a common image. A mirror with rust is a negative trope as it implies a lack of clarity.

Eternal Pit

sea's abyss— The ocean or sea can have many connotations, including generosity and the many iterations of existence (through the transformation of the sea to cloud, then to raindrop, then to the sea again). Just as often, the ocean is a site of danger and chaos, as it is in this poem.

A Story

budding smile— The link between smiling lips and the flower is most explicit in descriptions of roses opening, e.g., Mir Taqi Mir: "'How long is the life of a rose?' / The bud heard my question and smiled."

scorpion— With their black color and curling tails, scorpions can represent a beloved's entrancing black tresses. This hardly seems to be the case in this poem. Instead, the scorpion here is a source of potential contamination and death.

thunder, clouds, lightning— These often go hand in hand in Persian poetry, functioning in different ways to both signal (through thunder) and to precipitate (through lightning's soil-benefitting fire, the cloud's rain) spring and rejuvenation.

My Garden

In this translation, the ghazal's repetition ("I will") falls at the beginning of the line.

moonlight— The moon is often a metaphor for a beautiful face, but generally considered a thoroughly positive entity (a source of light in darkness).

shadow— This is often a force of misfortune. In this case, the speaker wants to use moonlight (a force of good) to turn the shadow into a positive entity. Shade can also have a positive connotation as a place that is cool and protected, and/or can suggest humility and commitment for its constant attachment to the earth.

I will gild every book— Anjuman boasts of her writing ability in this final stanza—a common gesture in Persian poetry.

Accept the Truth

hair— Hair or tresses as a means of capturing a beloved is a common trope. The hair can be like a lasso, or its curls can become linked chains, e.g., Kalim, *Dīwān*, ghazal no. 279: "Don't hunt flies; don't bind the heart of lustful people / with the snare of the tress which can bind angels!"

candle— The candle in Persian poetry often represents death or fate—or a beloved ("like a moth to the flame").

Korah— A figure of rabbinical literature who discovered one of the treasures Joseph hid in Egypt, gaining incredible wealth.

Nimrod— A Biblical king who famously ordered the construction of the Tower of Babel.

Haatam— A legendary man famous for his generosity.

Fresh Buds

earth— The earth is frequently connected to humility and reliability, but can take on a more positive or negative quality depending on its state (e.g., as plentiful or barren).

yellow— Yellow denotes human suffering, particularly in describing the pallor of the face, as it implies hunger.

Poison

scorpion— See note under "A Story" above.

My World

monochrome— A characteristic ("one color") in Persian culture that implies a lack of duplicitousness.

Drink! Drink!

In this translation, the ghazal's repetition ("why") falls at the beginning of the line.

tear your clothes— Tearing one's clothes is usually a gesture of protest, grief, or extreme sadness.

cage— The image of the cage implies that the person being addressed is like a captured bird.

Prison

cypress— The cypress is a recurring image in Persian verse, usually associated with a beloved for its beauty, height, and elegance. It is also connected to liberty, as it is a non-fruiting evergreen, unrestricted by progeny and never withering. Its height is connected to the story of the prophet Zoroaster planting a cypress in Kâshmar that, according to legend, grew to an incredible size.

Crazy Heart

In this translation, the ghazal's repetition ("I want") falls at the beginning of the line.

garden— The garden here is associated with Paradise.

water and seeds— These are sustenance for birds and often linked in a single image.

moth— The image of the moth, often burnt, is a common trope, frequently likened to the nightingale for its similar coloring. Above all it denotes a doomed romance or attachment, e.g., Shams-i Tabrizi, *Maqālāt*, 181: "The moth went after the light and fell in the fire." The moth is in love with a candle, but will ultimately burn its wings if it gets too close. This is considered a pure sacrifice for absolute and faithful love—the fire being the beloved, the moth the despondent lover.

Plaything

There is a rhyme scheme in this poem that we were unable to capture in English.

gold cups— Cups are often associated with wine, drunkenness, and revelry. Gold is ascribed to beauty and value. Here, the doll's box holds a status equivalent to gold cups.

tulip— Red and abundant throughout Iran and Afghanistan, the tulip is often called up to denote nature's beauty, e.g., Rashid-i-Watwat, *Dīwān*: "The border of greenery became filled with radiance because of the tulips; / The mouth of the tulips became filled with glittering pearls because of the dew." The tulip is also considered an image of bodily beauty, in contrast to the rose's beauty of the soul. Finally, due to their blood-red color, tulips are associated with martyrdom (as seems to be the case in this poem).

Bitter Stories

yellow— See note under "Fresh Buds" above.

Nimrod— See note under "Accept the Truth" above. Nimrod is often associated with tyranny and idolatry in the Jewish, Muslim, and Christian traditions. The unnamed Pharaoh in this poem also points to a tyrant figure.

The Night of Poetry

In this translation, the ghazal's repetition ("my") usually falls at the near-end of the line.

The Night of Poetry— The title refers to a cultural practice in which people gather and recite poems, often by others they admire.

pigeon— The pigeon (or at times nightingale) implies devotion, often to a beloved.

Mahshar— The gathering place of mankind on the day of judgment in Islam. Mahshar has a positive connotation. Alternatively, the term is used for a large and happy gathering.

Morning, don't tear at the silk— The image of the shiny black silk of night, lifted or removed by dawn, is a frequently used poetic image.

The Sun of Knowledge

While it may appear that each two lines repeat in Persian, there is actually a subtle rhyme scheme in the original. Some lines involve repetition of small words/phrases, which frequently fall at the beginning of the lines in English, rather than the end (as in the original).

wine— A defining image of Sufi poetry, with Sufis generally associating the intoxication from wine with the drunken love one feels for God.

A Taste of Ghazal

my heart opens— This is a specific idiom in Persian that implies growing happy.

Steel Strings

In this translation, the ghazal's repetition ("my") falls at the near-end or beginning of the line.

rose— Roses can bear a multitude of meanings, both spiritual and secular, including the figure of a bride, the beloved's face, a cup of wine, rubies, duplicity (beauty with thorns), as well as associations with the Prophet. Generally, roses are associated with love, particularly with the bulbul songbird, which poets often describe as a forlorn lover whose tears adorn the rose's petals with dew. In comparison to other beautiful flowers, the rose refers to the beauty of the spirit more frequently than that of the body.

the city of elegy and ghazals— Anjuman is referencing Herat, her home city, known for its centuries-long lineage of notable Persian and Sufi poets.

Flower of Smoke

The title in Persian, *Gul-e-Dodi*, may refer to a major crossroads in Herat named *Gul* ("Flower"), where the Taliban would often hang their victims.

It is a rare flower— A metaphor connecting a rose's petals to the bound leaves of a book is a recurring one.

Plea

At the time this poem was written, Afghanistan was experiencing a severe drought that lasted nearly a decade. This poem is an example of *tanâsob* ("harmony of imagery"), as Anjuman mentions three of the four natural elements.

rain— A sign of mercy as it provides much-needed water to dry earth.

I Wish

In this translation, the ghazal's repetition ("I wish I were") falls at the beginning of the line.

perfumed hair— The perfume Anjuman refers to is a specific kind of black musk made from the coagulated blood of a musk deer and used to perfume hair. This scent was often a poet's means of locating their goal or destination. The image of a beloved with black perfumed hair implies a particularly bewitching person.

Unnoticed

The italicized lines are quotations from a poem by Sayed Ziaulhaq Sakhaa (a contemporary poet living in Herat) entitled "Bloody Secret," which Anjuman sets after every three of her own lines in this poem. The form of "Unnoticed" is complicated. In the original Persian there is a rhyming or repetition of small words and phrases ("didn't," "we," "have been," etc.). These repetitions frequently fall at the beginning of these translated lines, rather than the end as in the original.

torn their clothes— See note under "My World" above.

cypress— See note under "Prison" above.

the grass wove her dresses— Nature weaving a beautiful fabric for the earth is a common trope.

tulip— See note under "Plaything" above.

Like Flint

In this translation, the ghazal's repetition ("me") is often in the middle of the line.

seeds and traps— Anjuman here is likening the speaker to a bird who may be lured by seeds (a frequent image in Persian poems).

The Sun's Lance

sun— The sun's rays are frequently connected to swords, arrows, and life. The sun itself calls up imagery of majestical beauty and generosity.

"Seven Thrones"— Anjuman is likely referencing "Seven Thrones," a cycle of seven *mathnawīs* by the fifteenth-century Sufi poet Nur ad-Din Abd ar-Rahman Jami. Jami's poem's title is another name for the constellation Ursa Major.

moonlike beauty— "Piece of the moon" is a poetic phrase often ascribed to a particularly beautiful woman.

green— Associated with Paradise as well as Islam, green is imbued with positive connotations. It is linked with joy and eternal life, as well as suggesting something tender and fresh—verdant growth.

Bedroom

Laila— A semi-historical woman from a long, twelfth-century Persian poem by Nezāmi of Ganja. Laila's lover, Qays, goes insane after she marries another man. Qays is then given the new name of Majnun (meaning "demented/possessed"). Majnun goes into the desert, speaking only to animals; a gazelle's black eyes remind him of his beloved and birds make a nest of his hair.

Velvet— Velvet is associated with sleep (often in the phrase "the sleep of velvet").

God-Given Beauty

In this translation, the ghazal's repetition ("you" or "your") falls at the end or near-end of the line. This ghazal can be read as a love poem, but is just as likely to be operating in the mode of a courtly panegyric poem, historically written by Persian poets in praise of supporters or patrons.

the dawn of your face— God or the beloved's face as an equivalent to the sun (or moon) is a frequent poetic image. The sun and moon are both symbols of beauty.

Scheherazade— Scheherazade famously saved her own life by telling remarkable stories to Shahryar in *One Thousand and One Nights*.

you are the dew … the spring morning's wind— The relationship between flowers, the morning's breeze, and dew is often associated with profound love.

The Most Faded Word

In this translation, the ghazal's repetition ("can't") falls at the near-end of the line.

burnt wings of a moth— See note under "Crazy Heart" above.

cypress— See note under "Prison" above. The cypress, so frequently associated with the stature and graceful movements of the beloved, is heartbreakingly destroyed here in a way that ruins specifically these two attributes.

don't breathe on me— The life-giving breath of the Messiah is a frequent image.

Escape

In this translation, the ghazal's repetition ("we," "our") falls at the beginning or near-beginning of these lines.

We Must Try

owl— A sinister image, as it is associated with ruins, where owls often live. There is also the potential connotation of greed, as owls reside in places of former glory and wealth, where one may find treasure.

Flower's pearly glow— Morning dew is frequently described as "pearls."

Pines— like cypresses (see note under "Prison" above), pines often connote a beloved's beauty and form.

eagle— Eagles are frequently associated with strength and violence, in contrast to the usual songbird.

white— White is an adjective that makes whatever it describes a positive entity. While we maintain it here, throughout the collection where you read "silver" or "silvery" as adjectives, the original is often more literally "white."

The Leaves of Patience

In this translation, the ghazal's repetition ("finally") this falls at the beginning of the line. This poem was likely written just after the fall of the Taliban in November 2001.

sun's rays— See note under "The Sun's Lance" above.

Turmoil

seeing with the heart's eye— This is a specific idiom that implies insight.

which strong hand should I look to— Looking at someone's hand implies an expectation or hope that they will provide something.

The Most Solemn Verse

In this translation, the ghazal's repetition ("I become") falls at the beginning or end of the line.

I become woven— In weaving, horizontal threads are woven through vertical threads. The vertical strands are called "warp" threads, the horizontal "weft." Anjuman uses this imagery, stating that with a little hope the speaker will become the weft threads woven through the already-present warp threads of the heart and produce a fabric or tapestry. The warp and weft elements of weaving recur frequently in Persian verse, suggesting everything from the divine to the death shroud, e.g., Farrukhi Sistani, *qaṣīda* no. 169: "Each thread of its warp twisted by the spirit with pain, / each thread in its weft cut from the heart."

Further Reading

Dick Davis (tr. and ed.), *The Mirror of My Heart: A Thousand Years of Persian Poetry by Women*. New York: Penguin Random House, 2021.

Forough Farrokhzad, *Let Us Believe in the Beginning of the Cold Season*. Tr. Elizabeth T. Gray, Jr. New York: New Directions, 2022.

Anand Gopal, *No Good Men Among the Living: America, the Taliban, and the War Through Afghan Eyes*. New York: Henry Holt, 2014.

Eliza Griswold and Seamus Murphy, *I Am the Beggar of the World: Landays from Contemporary Afghanistan*. New York: Farrar, Straus and Giroux, 2014.

Christina Lamb, *The Sewing Circles of Herat: A Personal Voyage Through Afghanistan*. New York: Harper Perennial, 2004.

Annemarie Schimmel, *A Two-Colored Brocade: The Imagery of Persian Poetry*. Chapel Hill: University of North Carolina Press, 2004.

Åsne Seierstad, *The Afghans: Three Lives Through War, Love, and Revolt*. New York: Bloomsbury, 2025.

Ali-Asghar Seyed-Ghorab (ed.), *The Layered Heart: Essays on Persian Poetry*. Washington, D.C.: Mage Publishers, 2018.

——. *Metaphor and Imagery in Persian Poetry*. Leiden, Netherlands: Brill Publishers, 2011.

Acknowledgments

The translations included in this volume were previously published in the following journals: Apogee, Arc Poetry Magazine, Asymptote, Aufgabe, Brooklyn Rail, Circumference, Denver Quarterly, Eleven Eleven, Exchanges Journal, Gulf Coast, International Poetry Review, National Translation Month, North American Review, Poet Lore, Two Lines. The poems "A Taste of Ghazal," "If," "My Garden," "Prison," and "Plaything" were included in the anthology Hair on Fire: Afghan Women Poets, published in the Calico Series by Two Lines Press in 2025.

Our gratitude to the editors and staff members of the above publications for their tireless work in supporting translators and the greater translation community.

Thank you to Jen Hofer who, from the start, supported me through this complex project. Thank you to Marina, my partner through this whole process—I'm so grateful for your friendship! Thank you to Yvette Siegert who gave her remarkable eye to these poems; to Fariba Sirjani for going through the manuscript so closely; to Saboor Siasang for copy editing.

In addition, I'm grateful to Dena Afrasiabi, Allison M. Charette, Gabrielle Civil, Katrina Dodson, Barbara Epler, Reena Esmail, Nuno Gomes, Elizabeth T. Gray, Jr., Regina Guimarães, Umair Kazi and the Author's Guild staff, Amir Mashayekhi, Farzana Marie, Erica Mena, Sawako Nakayasu, Jennifer Nelson, Zohra Saed, Fatemeh Shams, and others who have provided guidance throughout the fifteen years it took to translate, edit, and publish this collection.

One of the greatest gifts of working on Anjuman's poetry has been becoming a member of the supportive community of literary translators I so cherish. My deepest gratitude to the American Literary Translators Association and its staff for its annual conference, which made it possible for me to befriend such remarkable, giving, and thoughtful people. I have never felt so effortlessly accepted into a community. I could not have continued this work without them.

Thank you to the Banff Literary Centre and Yaddo residencies. This translation was made possible by the Diploma of Innovation Grant from the University of Southern California.

Thank you to the wonderful staff at World Poetry Books for their important work in the niche-but-vital literature of poetry in translation. I am so grateful this volume found its home with you.

And, finally, to S., Anjuman's brother, for the deep honor of his trust in our work. May this translation be the first of many.

[D.A.]

Biographies

Born in Herat, Afghanistan, **Nadia Anjuman** (1980-2005) surreptitiously gathered with women in the Golden Needle School to discuss literature under the guise of practicing needlepoint—one of the few Taliban-approved pastimes for women. After Afghanistan's liberation from the Taliban, Anjuman attended Herat University and published *Gul-e-Dodi* (Flower of Smoke). She died in 2005 after being severely beaten by her husband. Her second volume of poetry, *Yek Sàbad Délhoreh* (A Basket of Doubt), was published the following year. *Flower of Smoke* has been reprinted three times and sold over three thousand copies with readers in Iran, Pakistan, France, and beyond. Her poetry has since been translated and published in Italian and Portuguese.

Diana Arterian holds a PhD in Literature & Creative Writing from the University of Southern California and is the author of the poetry collections *Agrippina the Younger* (Northwestern University Press) and *Playing Monster :: Seiche* (1913 Press). Her work has been recognized with fellowships from the Banff Centre, Caldera, Millay Arts, Vermont Studio Center, and Yaddo. A Poetry Editor at Noemi Press, she writes "The Annotated Nightstand" column at *Lit Hub* and lives in Los Angeles.

Marina Omar moved to the U.S. from Afghanistan in 2001 and received her PhD from the University of Virginia in Political Science in 2016. Marina has published an article on Afghan constitution selection in *British Journal of Middle Eastern Studies*. Her research has been supported by multiple fellowships and grants, including The Buckner W. Clay Endowment for the Humanities Fellowship, The Robert J. Huskey Travel Fellowship, and Quandt International Research Fund. She has taught at the University of Virginia, Mary Washington University, and Mary Baldwin University.

Aria Aber grew up in Germany, where she was born to Afghan refugees. Her poetry collection *Hard Damage* (University of Nebraska Press), won the Prairie Schooner Book Prize in Poetry and a Whiting Award. A graduate of the NYU MFA in Creative Writing, she holds awards and fellowships from Kundiman, the Wisconsin Institute of Creative Writing, and the Wallace Stegner Fellowship at Stanford University. Her first novel, *Good Girl*, was recently published by Hogarth. She is a contributing editor at *The Yale Review*, and an assistant professor of Creative Writing at the University of Vermont.

The Persian in this book was typeset in Markazi Text, a contemporary multi-script family designed by Borna Izadpanah and Florian Runge in 2017 as a joint project of the University of Reading and Google. The English was set in Nassim Latin, designed by Titus Nemeth for Rosetta Type Foundry, Brno. Cover design by Andrew Bourne. Typesetting by Don't Look Now. Printed and bound in Lithuania by BALTO Print. Manufactured by Arctic Paper in Sweden, the paper in this book meets EU Ecolabel, Forest Stewardship Council, and Cradle to Cradle certification standards.

# WORLD POETRY

Samer Abu Hawwash
Ruins and Other Poems
tr. Huda J. Fakhreddine

Marie-Noëlle Agniau
The Escapades
tr. Jesse Hover Amar

Nadia Anjuman
Smoke Drifts:
Selected Poems
tr. Diana Arterian
& Marina Omar

Jean-Paul Auxeméry
Selected Poems
tr. Nathaniel Tarn

Leire Bilbao
Fish Scales: Selected Poems
tr. Joana Urtasun

Boethius
The Poems from On the
Consolation of Philosophy
tr. Peter Glassgold

Maria Borio
Transparencies
tr. Danielle Pieratti

Astrid Cabral
Spotlight on the Word
tr. Alexis Levitin

Jeannette L. Clariond
Goddesses of Water
tr. Samantha Schnee

Jacques Darras
John Scotus Eriugena
at Laon
tr. Richard Sieburth

Mario dell'Arco
Day Lasts Forever:
Selected Poems
tr. Marc Alan Di Martino

Marie de Quatrebarbes
The Vitals
tr. Aiden Farrell

Ricardo Domeneck
First Epistle to the
Amphibians: Selected Poems
tr. Chris Daniels

Olivia Elias
Chaos, Crossing
tr. Kareem James Abu-Zeid

Gastón Fernández
Apparent Breviary
tr. KM Cascia

Jerzy Ficowski
Everything I Don't Know
tr. Jennifer Grotz
& Piotr Sommer
PEN AWARD FOR POETRY IN
TRANSLATION

Antonio Gamoneda
Book of the Cold
tr. Katherine M. Hedeen &
Víctor Rodríguez Núñez

Mireille Gansel
Soul House
tr. Joan Seliger Sidney

Óscar García Sierra
Houston, I'm the problem
tr. Carmen Yus Quintero

Phoebe Giannisi
Homerica
tr. Brian Sneeden

Zuzanna Ginczanka
On Centaurs & Other Poems
tr. Alex Braslavsky

Julien Gracq
Abounding Freedom
tr. Alice Yang

Karmelo C. Iribarren
You've Heard This One
Before: Selected Poems
tr. John R. Sesgo

Leeladhar Jagoori
What of the Earth
Was Saved
tr. Matt Reeck

Nakedness Is My End:
Poems from the Greek
Anthology
tr. Edmund Keeley

Birhan Keskin
Earthly Conditions:
Selected Poems
tr. Öykü Tekten

Jazra Khaleed
The Light That Burns Us
ed. Karen Van Dyck

Judith Kiros
O
tr. Kira Josefsson

Dimitra Kotoula
The Slow Horizon
That Breathes
tr. Maria Nazos

Maria Laina
Hers
tr. Karen Van Dyck

Maria Laina
Rose Fear
tr. Sarah McCann

Perrin Langda
A Few Microseconds on
Earth
tr. Pauline Levy Valensi

Anna Malihon
Girl with a Bullet
tr. Olena Jennings

Afrizal Malna
Document Shredding
Museum
tr. Daniel Owen

Joyce Mansour
In the Glittering Maw:
Selected Poems
tr. C. Francis Fisher

Manuel Maples Arce
Stridentist Poems
tr. KM Cascia

Selma Meerbaum-Eisinger
Song of the Yellow Asters
tr. Carlie Hoffman

Ennio Moltedo
Night
tr. Marguerite Feitlowitz

Meret Oppenheim
The Loveliest Vowel Empties:
Collected Poems
tr. Kathleen Heil

Giovanni Pascoli
Last Dream
tr. Geoffrey Brock
RAIZISS/DE PALCHI
TRANSLATION AWARD

Gabriel Pomerand
Saint Ghetto of the Loans
tr. Michael Kasper &
Bhamati Viswanathan

Liliana Ponce
Theory of the Voice and Dream
tr. Michael Martin Shea

Rainer Maria Rilke
Where the Paths Do Not Go
tr. Burton Pike

Amelia Rosselli
Document
tr. Roberta Antognini
& Deborah Woodard

Elisabeth Rynell
Night Talks
tr. Rika Lesser

Waly Salomão
Border Fare
tr. Maryam Monalisa Gharavi

George Sarantaris
Abyss and Song:
Selected Poems
tr. Pria Louka

George Seferis
Book of Exercises II
tr. Jennifer R. Kellogg
ELIZABETH CONSTANTINIDES
MEMORIAL TRANSLATION PRIZE

Seo Jung Hak
The Cheapest France in Town
tr. Megan Sungyoon

Ahmad Shamlou
Elegies of the Earth:
Selected Poems
tr. Niloufar Talebi

Edith Södergran
Modern Woman
tr. CD Eskilson

Ardengo Soffici
Simultaneities &
Lyric Chemisms
tr. Olivia E. Sears

Liesl Ujvary
Good & Safe
tr. Ann Cotten &
Anna-Isabella Dinwoodie

Paul Verlaine
Before Wisdom:
The Early Poems
tr. Keith Waldrop
& K.A. Hays

Haris Vlavianos
Renaissance
tr. Patricia Barbeito

Witold Wirpsza
Apotheosis of Music
tr. Frank L. Vigoda

Uljana Wolf
kochanie, today i bought bread
tr. Greg Nissan

Ye Lijun
My Mountain Country
tr. Fiona Sze-Lorrain

Verónica Zondek
Cold Fire
tr. Katherine Silver